# Books by Robert Ackart

SOUFFLÉS, MOUSSES, JELLIES & CREAMS    1980

CHEESE    1978

A CELEBRATION OF VEGETABLES    1977

THE ONE-DISH COOKBOOK    1975

COOKING IN A CASSEROLE    1973

FRUITS IN COOKING    1973

100 MENU CHICKEN COOKBOOK    1972

# Soufflés, Mousses,
# Jellies & Creams

# Soufflés, Mousses,

DRAWINGS BY MARJORIE ZAUM

# Robert Ackart

# Jellies & Creams

New York   1980   Atheneum

Library of Congress Cataloging in Publication Data

Ackart, Robert C
  Soufflés, mousses, jellies, and creams.
  Includes index.
  1. Soufflés. 2. Mousses. 3. Cookery (Molded
dishes) I. Title.
TX773.A28        641.8'2        79-55606
ISBN 0-689-11028-6

Published simultaneously in Canada by
  McClelland and Stewart Ltd.
Manufactured by American Book–Stratford Press, Inc.,
  Saddle Brook, New Jersey
Designed by Kathleen Carey
First Edition

*For Errol Anthony Chin-Loy*

———————————

# Introduction

This book is the result of my pleasure in making these original and festive dishes; I have written it simply because I want to share my enthusiasm.

Soufflés (which include mousses), jellies (which include aspics), and creams (which include ice creams)—at first encounter a rather diverse collection, a culinary mixed bag, as it were. Not really, for the dishes have in common several attractive qualities. As cousins from the kitchen, they all "eat easily." Their possible textural variations are many, from the pleasant crunch of a fresh vegetable mousse to the satin smoothness of chocolate *pots de crème*. In a way, they are related by their very diversity; few dishes are capable of such varied tastes as these which may be made with virtually any ingredient you care to use: from artichokes to yams, avocados to strawberries, chicken to lamb to sole filets.

Because of current eating habits, which tend to minimize use of sweets, rather fewer recipes for dessert soufflés and jellies are included than for main dishes, the principal focus of the book. Creams, by their nature, are desserts, but effort has been made to keep their number and dietary influence under control by offering carefully selected ones. (The desserts are only pleasantly sweetened and are quite often tart.)

Why soufflés and jellies as the principal focus of the meal?

First, because we increasingly eat "light." Few of us enjoy feeling sated by food; the postprandial stupor described in nineteenth-century novels is no longer our way of life. No dish is more satisfying but less leaden than a soufflé or jelly or, if properly prepared, a dessert cream.

Each is nourishing and refreshing. Each leaves the eater with the feeling that, while having more would be enjoyable, the meal has been whole and complete.

A second attractive quality of main-dish soufflés and jellies lies in their aesthetic appeal. A molded mousse, its center filled with accompanying food of complementary flavor, color, and texture, a well-puffed, golden soufflé, or a sparkling, cool aspic—all are tempting to look at. They are elegant and stylish dishes. In warm weather, they are cool to the palate; in all seasons, their smoothness is inviting. In all seasons, too, they bring a gala ambiance to the dining table. They are fun to make, fun to offer (their appearance at table is invariably a conversation starter—or stopper), and fun to eat.

A third reason for my enthusiasm about these dishes lies in their ease of preparation. I am a sociable cook and prefer being with family or friends than packed off to work in the kitchen. Cold soufflés (made with gelatin as presented in this book), jellies, and creams may be made well in advance of serving: in the morning for the evening meal, or a full day ahead, even two days if they are carefully covered with plastic wrap. Hot soufflés and mousses may be prepared up to the point of beating the egg whites and folding them into the batter, at most a ten-minute job, after which the dish goes into a preheated oven to emerge in 30 to 45 minutes with all the glamour you intended for it.

The baking dish or mold may be buttered ahead; the old saw about leaving the dish dry in order that the soufflé have "something to climb on" is, I feel, hokum. I rarely put a soufflé dish in a pan of hot water when baking the final product—another superstition, I believe, and another instance of unorthodoxy on my part—*except* when the recipe directs doing so, as is the case with hot mousses. The success of soufflé- and mousse-making lies only in having everything ready and at room temperature and then working not fast but steadily.

A fourth pleasure I take in soufflés and jellies is a very practical one: They are economical. Eggs, their first principal ingredient, are certainly less costly than meat. Vegetables and fruits, their second principal ingredient, are finding increasing favor among dollar-wise homemakers who are newly discovering their wide variety of flavors and textures—a variety far exceeding that of meat dishes. When meats are listed as the second principal ingredient, they are most frequently leftovers—save in the case of fish or seafood—and hence another economic plus in the mind of the cook.

Each section of the book starts with a basic recipe for the dish concerned (main-dish soufflés, cold main-dish mousses, etc.), followed by a number of variations made possible by the use of different principal ingredients or seasonings. Then, because all recipes are not conformable to a basic recipe, complete recipes for "nonconformist" dishes follow.

Fresh vegetables and fruits are the preferred ingredients of these recipes, but frozen ones are satisfactory; and, yes, some canned ones, too. Recipes list the fresh ingredient first and, second, recommend a frozen or canned substitute. I have arranged the recipes this way because I enjoy using fresh produce whenever possible, but when these are unavailable, the dependability of frozen or canned foods is indeed a comfort. Certain canned products, such as beets or pumpkin purée, are remarkably like the fresh product in both taste and texture, and they boast the great advantage of being time-saving. When their use is indicated, I have no qualms in listing them. I do urge that fresh produce be cooked in a minimum of water and only until tender-crisp; prepared in this way, it retains its color, flavor, and nutritional properties.

Of practical concern to the meal-planner is the appeal of these dishes to the finicky eater, not only because of their appetizing appearance, but also because of the beneficial nourishment which belies their airy lightness and shimmering coolness. These same qualities, it should be added, make soufflés and jellies ideal fare for the diner with delicate digestion or for someone actually unwell.

Are not soufflés and mousses fattening, high in cholesterol, etc., etc.? No, they are not fattening, any more than is a baked potato if eaten simply. It is our combinations of foods which make for fattening diets. True, soufflés are prepared with eggs, but at an equivalency of never more than one per serving, and often less than that. In any case, it is not intended that the reader eat soufflé every day; the book proposes soufflés for your pleasure in the kitchen and at table, rather than as a dietary regimen.

Cold dessert soufflés and mousses are most often made with whipped cream; they are light, but they are rich, too. For this reason, and also because, hot or cold, they do contain some sugar, I suggest that dessert soufflés and mousses serve six to eight. (Numerous dessert mousses are suggested in which only beaten egg white provides the characteristic bouyancy.) Main-dish soufflés and mousses yield four generous servings. Recipes for aspics and dessert jellies and creams serve six to eight persons.

No cookbook is written by one person alone; recipes are tested on family and friends whose votes of yea or nay or whose suggestions, later incorporated in the dish, are valuable to the author. I extend warm thanks, therefore, to family and friends for their perceptive and frequently corrective palates. Most especially, however, I am beholden to my esteemed friend Lola Wilson Hayes, who for several years has spent summer vacations at my home in Katonah. At such times, she is not a captive audience, but rather a captive guinea pig, culinarily speaking. The number of soufflés, mousses, jellies, and creams to which she has been subjected in the name of this book far exceeds the demands of appetite or good humor or friendship. Much of my joy in writing the book is due to her and, if it proves useful and enjoyable to the reader, these qualities directly reflect her enthusiastic encouragement and interest.

Join me now in the inventive and pleasurable preparation of soufflés, mousses, jellies, and creams. I have had such satisfaction in evolving these recipes that I feel I offer not another cookbook, but a little of my own way of living, which I am happy to share with you.

Robert Ackart

Katonah, New York
1979

# Contents

---

I  SOUFFLES AND MOUSSES  1

HOT MAIN-DISH SOUFFLÉS AND MOUSSES  3

COLD MAIN-DISH MOUSSES  47

HOT DESSERT SOUFFLÉS  68

COLD DESSERT SOUFFLÉS AND MOUSSES  82

II  JELLIES  111

MAIN-DISH JELLIES  114

GELATIN DESSERTS  139

III  CREAMS AND ICE CREAMS  155

IV  A FEW SAUCES AND SALADS  187

INDEX  199

# Soufflés and Mousses

# Hot Main-Dish Soufflés and Mousses

## The All-Important Egg

Whether the recipe calls for the whole egg or for the white only, eggs are the *sine qua non* of soufflés and mousses; without them, neither dish can be made. Because eggs are the *prime donne* of these operas, it behooves the cook, as *chef d'orchestre*, to treat them with respect, tender loving care, and to know a little about them.

The calorie count of one large egg is 77. A one-quarter-pound ground-round hamburger, broiled (not pan-fried with butter), is 220 calories. The egg costs about 8⅓ cents; the meat patty about 45. The white of egg is composed of about 88% water and 12% protein; the yolk, of about 49% water, 19% protein, and 32% fat. Egg proteins supply all necessary amino acids and most essential minerals, in addition to vitamins A and D and riboflavin. The beef patty is composed of about 59% water, 25% protein, and 15% fat. It supplies, like the egg, phosphorus and iron, as well as traces of niacin.

Is there, perhaps, a lesson to be gleaned from these facts?

Soufflés and mousses are most successfully made, hot or cold, with *very* fresh U.S. grade "A" large or extra-large eggs, the extra-large giving more white in proportion to the size of the yolk. Both soufflés and mousses are enhanced by the addition of an extra white or two. Eggs perform best at room temperature; indeed, the time and effort needed to beat egg whites until stiff can be nearly halved by removing the eggs from the refrigerator an hour or two beforehand.

Do not use aluminum utensils when cooking with eggs. Because of their sulphur content, both yolks and whites discolor when mixed, cooked, or molded in aluminum. I recommend utensils of stainless steel, ovenproof glass or porcelain, or tin-lined copper. Speaking of copper, there *is* truth in the rumor that a copper bowl is first-rate for beating egg whites; there exists a sort of chemistry between the bowl and its contents which makes for quicker and higher rising of the egg white; this is especially true if you beat with a wire whisk. Any bowl or beater, however, is serviceable.

Beaten egg white will not stand for any length of time. Once fallen, it cannot be resuscitated. For main-dish or savory soufflés, a few drops of lemon juice, one-half teaspoonful of cream of tartar, or one table-spoonful of white vinegar, added before the whites are beaten, will help to hold them. For dessert soufflés, the addition of one tablespoonful of sugar after the whites have been beaten frothy will serve the same purpose. Covering the beaten egg white with a tight seal of plastic wrap and refrigerating it extends its life, but only momentarily. Beaten egg white lives on transient breath at best and, indeed, will not beat stiff at all if there is the slightest bit of yolk in it. Remove any noxious drop of yolk with a piece of egg shell or piece of paper towel, to which the yolk seems disposed to adhere. To avoid any of the yolk's sneak-ing into the white, break each egg separately, parting yolk from white as you do so, and, before breaking the next egg, transfer the untainted white to the bowl in which the combined whites will be beaten.

Unbeaten egg whites store very well. They may be frozen "in bulk" and, if necessary, thawed and then refrozen. Individual ice-cube molds hold just about the white of one egg; thus you can see easily how many spares you have on hand. Egg yolks, however, do not freeze; they can be refrigerated for several days, tightly sealed from air.

Having become acquainted with the leading lady of soufflés and mousses, let us turn to the dishes themselves. A soufflé—its name is the French word for "inflated" or "puffed"—or mousse—its name is the French word for "foam"—can stand as the main dish of the meal or as dessert. Soufflés require both the yolk and white of the egg; some mousses are prepared with the white only.

Originally soufflés were hot dishes, savory or sweet; now, however, the name is also applied to cold desserts which are really creams. A savory or main-dish soufflé is, simply, a baked egg dish based on a thick *béchamel* or "cream" sauce with ingredients added for flavor and texture, and beaten egg whites. The *béchamel* is made from a *roux*:

equal amounts of fat (usually butter but not always so) and flour, cooked together over gentle heat to rid the flour of its raw taste and to expand its cells so that it may combine smoothly with milk.

A hot sweet or dessert soufflé is made from either a *béchamel* or a fruit base. In the preparation of hot soufflés, whether savory or sweet, the height to which the baked recipe rises and its airiness are direct results of how the egg whites have been beaten; they should be very stiff but not dry, as I explain on page 6.

Most hot mousses "hold" before serving without threat of their falling; a hot soufflé *should* go direct from oven to table, but all is not necessarily lost if it does not (see page 6). A hot mousse should stand at room temperature for 5 minutes before being unmolded; during this time it will set and shrink slightly from the sides of its mold, making its *unmolding* considerably easier.

But now let us move on to the making of hot soufflés and mousses: to this end, here follow six specifics which will assure you of producing these delectable dishes with a sense of carefree enjoyment and adventure.

*Specific I:* Assemble *all* the utensils you will need: measuring cups and spoons, mixing spoon, wire whisk or rotary beater (manual or electric), a rubber spatula; a saucepan (one of 3-quart capacity will accommodate the folding in of the egg white, Specific V, below), a bowl in which to beat the egg whites, and an ovenproof dish or dishes in which to bake the soufflé, or a mold for the mousse.

Assemble and prepare the ingredients called for in the recipe. Measure out the butter, flour, and milk. Soufflés are more easily and successfully made when all ingredients are at room temperature.

*Specific II:* Thoroughly butter the soufflé dish or hot-mousse mold: one generous tablespoonful of butter is sufficient. If you want a crusty soufflé, dust the buttered dish with fine bread crumbs or a very dry grated cheese such as Parmesan.

Having done this much, you may, if you wish, stop and continue later. Or (and this is my practice) you may prepare the batter *up to but not including* the beating of the egg whites. In other words, you may complete the recipe to the point at which it calls for "egg whites, beaten until stiff but not dry." Cover the prepared batter with the lid of the saucepan or with plastic wrap (you will note that the entire mixture may be prepared in this single utensil), leave it at room temperature, stop, and continue later.

*Specific III:* Upon resuming preparation, which you should do only when you are ready to bake the recipe, turn on the oven to the designated temperature; make sure it has reached proper heat before continuing.

*Specific IV:* Beat the egg whites in your preferred way: with a whisk, with a beater, in a copper bowl, in another sort of bowl—it really does not matter. The whites should be stiff but not dry; in other words, they should stand in satiny peaks, look "wet," and adhere to the beater when it is held straight up. They become grainy if overbeaten and will not fold evenly into the batter. As has been suggested, soufflés are always improved by the addition of an extra egg white or two, although such addition is not necessary.

*Specific V:* Into the prepared batter, beat about one-fifth of the egg white; then, using a rubber spatula, fold the remaining egg white into the contents of the saucepan. Do *not* stir horizontally; doing so will deflate the egg white. Folding mixes by moving the spatula with a vertical motion down, then along the bottom of the saucepan toward you, and, finally, drawing it up and back toward the side of the saucepan opposite you. This procedure, which seems complicated in print, is very easy in practice; before long you will be able to rotate the saucepan as you do it, a measure ensuring smooth folding.

Using the rubber spatula, transfer the batter to the prepared dish. To assure even distribution of heat, bake it as directed, on a rack in the middle of the oven. A soufflé in a 2-quart dish usually bakes at 350° Fahrenheit for 30 minutes; a mousse in a 5- or 6-cup ring mold usually bakes in a pan of hot water at 375° Fahrenheit for 40 minutes; individual soufflés usually bake at 400° Fahrenheit for 15 to 20 minutes. Variances in these timings are given in particular recipes.

*Specific VI:* When a soufflé is well-puffed and golden at the end of the designated baking time, it should be served at once. If, however, its presentation is briefly delayed, merely turn off the oven; it will not cook appreciably more and will stay risen for 5 to 8 minutes. At the end of this time, serve! A linen napkin on a tray or large plate makes for a pleasant appearance and prevents the soufflé dish from sliding about if it is passed.

For the cook who wishes to offer a sauce complementary to hot main-dish soufflés and mousses, there are in Chapter IV a number of dressings; these sauces are a pleasant addition, but no sauce is a *must.* It is only an embellishment. If the soufflé or mousse is of especially delicate flavor, it is best to omit a sauce.

## Basic Recipe for Main-Dish Soufflés

4 SERVINGS

PREPARATION: APPROXIMATELY 30 MINUTES (THE PREPARATION TIME WILL
VARY DEPENDING UPON HOW MUCH READYING THE MAIN INGREDIENT
REQUIRES)

COOKING: 30 MINUTES IN A 350° OVEN

*All the ingredients may be readied ahead and combined according to
the directions at the time of cooking.*

Thoroughly butter a 2-quart soufflé dish.

**4 tablespoons butter**
**4 tablespoons flour**

In a saucepan, heat the butter and in it, over gentle heat, cook the
flour for a few minutes. This mixture is called a *roux.*

### Special seasonings

If the recipe calls for such special seasonings as ground spices, for example, add them to the *roux;* the butter in the *roux* will facilitate the
elimination of small lumps, which you will not want in the completed soufflé. (One of my favorite seasonings is chicken or vegetable
bouillon cubes, powdered, which often replaces salt in these recipes;
bouillon powder, stirred into the *roux,* enriches the delicate flavor of
soufflés.)

**1 cup milk**

Gradually add the milk, stirring constantly until the mixture is thickened and smooth. This mixture is call a *béchamel.*

### Prepared major ingredient*

Into the contents of the saucepan, blend the major ingredient (see
individual recipes below). Add or adjust the seasonings.

* Many recipes suggest adding the major ingredient *after* the addition of the egg
yolks; this method is fine if you prefer it. I recommend the procedure as stated
because stirring the main ingredient into the hot *béchamel* assures that the mixture
will be sufficiently cool not to cook the yolks *sur le champ,* as it were—another
of my unorthodoxies.

4 egg yolks

Beat in the egg yolks.

4 egg whites, beaten until stiff but not dry, page 6

Into the soufflé batter, beat one-fifth of the egg white; fold in the remainder. Using a rubber spatula, transfer the mixture to the prepared dish. Bake the soufflé according to the directions given above, or until it is well-puffed and golden.

ARTICHOKE SOUFFLÉ: Add 2 powdered bouillon cubes to the *roux*; gradually add the milk; season the *béchamel* with additional salt, if needed, and pepper; add 1 nine-ounce package of frozen artichoke hearts, fully thawed to room temperature and chopped fine; stir in ¼ cupful of grated Parmesan cheese. Complete the basic recipe as written.

ASPARAGUS SOUFFLÉ: Using 1 nine-ounce package of frozen asparagus, fully thawed to room temperature and chopped fine, will enable you to enjoy this soufflé year round. If you prefer, trim and cook for 10 minutes in a minimum of water 1 pound of fresh asparagus. Drain and chop it fine, reserving the cooking water. To the cooking water, add milk to equal 1 cup and use this liquid to make the *béchamel*. Season the *béchamel* with a few drops of Tabasco sauce and salt to taste. Add the asparagus and complete the basic recipe as written, baking the soufflé for 35 minutes.

BEET GREENS SOUFFLÉ: Follow the directions for Spinach Soufflé, page 14, using the greens from a 1-pound bunch of beets, boiled for 1 minute, pressed dry in a colander, and chopped fine (unless the beets are very young, discard the lower portion of the leaf stem). If desired, ¼ cupful of grated Parmesan cheese may be added to the *béchamel* with the beet greens. Complete the basic recipe as written.

BROCCOLI SOUFFLÉ: Trim and cook for 1 minute in lightly salted boiling water 1 pound of fresh broccoli; thoroughly drain and chop it fine. If you prefer, use 1 ten-ounce package of frozen chopped broccoli; cook it until just tender according to the directions on the package. To the *béchamel*, add the prepared broccoli and, if desired, ¼ cupful of grated Parmesan cheese. Complete the basic recipe as written.

BRUSSELS SPROUTS SOUFFLÉ: Use 1 pint of fresh brussels sprouts, trimmed and rinsed, *or* 1 ten-ounce package of frozen brussels sprouts; cook them in a minimum of lightly salted water for 10 minutes, until they are just tender; drain the sprouts, reserving ½ cupful of the liquid; chop them fine and reserve them. To the liquid, add milk to equal 1 cup; reserve it. To the *roux*, add 1 small onion, peeled and grated, and 2 powdered bouillon cubes. Make the *béchamel* with the reserved milk mixture; add the prepared Brussels sprouts and a few drops of Tabasco sauce. Complete the basic recipe as written.

CALF'S BRAINS SOUFFLÉ: Prepare 1 pound of calf's brains according to the directions for sweetbreads, page 15; reserve them. To the *roux*, add a grating of nutmeg. To the *béchamel*, add the reserved calf's brains, ¼ cupful of fine-chopped parsley, and salt and pepper to taste. Complete the basic recipe as written.

CARROT SOUFFLÉ: In boiling salted water to cover, cook 4 large carrots, scraped, for 15 minutes, or until they are just tender; drain and force them through a sieve or purée them in the container of a food processor; reserve the purée. To the *roux*, add a generous grating of nutmeg. To the *béchamel*, add the carrot purée, salt and pepper to taste. Complete the basic recipe as written.

CAULIFLOWER SOUFFLÉ: Cook, whole, 1 large cauliflower (about 1½ pounds) in 1 inch of boiling water until it is tender (18 to 20 minutes); drain and chop it coarse. In the container of a food processor or blender, combine the cauliflower and ¾ cupful of milk; whirl the mixture until it is smooth. Reserve it. To the *roux*, add 2 powdered bouillon cubes, a few grains of cayenne, and ½ teaspoonful of ground cumin. Make the *béchamel* with the reserved cauliflower-milk mixture; to it, add ¼ cupful of fine-chopped parsley and, if desired, ¼ cupful of grated Parmesan cheese. Complete the basic recipe as written, baking the soufflé at 350° for 40 minutes.

CELERIAC (CELERY ROOT) SOUFFLÉ: In lightly salted boiling water to cover, cook 1 one-pound bulb of celeriac, trimmed, peeled, and cut into ½-inch slices; when it is tender (about

20 minutes), drain and force the vegetable through a sieve or purée it in the container of a food processor; reserve the purée. To the *roux*, add 2 powdered bouillon cubes, ¼ teaspoonful of powdered cumin, and ¼ teaspoonful of white pepper. To the *béchamel*, add the celeriac purée. Complete the basic recipe as written, baking the soufflé at 375° for 30 minutes.

CELERY SOUFFLÉ: In a saucepan, heat 2 tablespoonfuls of butter and in it cook 2 cupfuls of diced celery for 8 minutes, or until it is just tender. To the *béchamel*, add the celery and salt and white pepper to taste. Complete the basic recipe as written.

CHEESE SOUFFLÉ: To the *béchamel*, add 1 cupful of Gruyère *or* Emmenthaler, grated coarse, *or* 1 cupful of grated Parmesan; add salt and white pepper to taste. Complete the basic recipe as written.

For *Brie* or *Camembert Soufflé*, stir into the hot *béchamel* 1 cupful of fine-diced Brie or Camembert cheese. Complete the basic ricipe as written.

CHESTNUT SOUFFLÉ: To the *roux*, add 2 powdered bouillon cubes and 1 small onion, peeled and grated. Make the *béchamel* with ¾ cupful of milk; to it, add 1 cupful of chestnut purée (available at specialty food shops), a few drops of Tabasco sauce, and salt to taste. Complete the basic recipe as written.

CHICKEN SOUFFLÉ: To the *roux*, add 2 powdered chicken bouillon cubes. To the *béchamel*, add 1 cupful of fine-minced or ground cooked chicken meat and ¼ cupful of fine-chopped parsley. Complete the basic recipe as written.

CHICKEN AND CLAM SOUFFLÉ: To the *roux*, add 2 powdered chicken bouillon cubes. To the liquid from 1 eight-ounce can of minced clams, thoroughly drained, add milk to equal 1 cup; use this mixture to make the *béchamel*. To the *béchamel*, add the reserved clams and 1 five-ounce can of boned chicken, thoroughly mashed with a fork. Complete the basic recipe as written.

CHICKEN LIVER SOUFFLÉ: Soak in cold salted water for 1 hour 1 pound of chicken livers, the membranes and fat removed;

drain them on absorbent paper and then purée in the container of a food processor or blender; reserve the purée. Make the *roux* with 5 tablespoonfuls of flour and to it add ½ teaspoonful of nutmeg. To the *béchamel*, add the chicken liver purée and season the mixture with salt and pepper to taste. Complete the basic recipe as written.

CHIPPED BEEF SOUFFLÉ: Shred and soak for 1 hour in cold water 1 four-ounce package of chipped beef; drain it and in the butter for the *roux*, over medium heat, sauté it until it is quite dry and "frizzled." Add the flour to complete the *roux* and, if desired, 1 small onion, peeled and grated. Add the milk gradually, stirring the mixture until it is thickened and smooth; stir in ⅓ cupful of fine-chopped parsley and a grinding of pepper to taste. Complete the basic recipe as written.

CLAM SOUFFLÉ: Drain 2 six-ounce cans of minced clams; to the liquid, add milk to equal 1 cup; reserve it and the clams. To the *roux*, add 1 small onion, peeled and grated. Make the *béchamel* with the reserved liquid; add the clams and ¼ cupful of fine-chopped parsley; season the mixture with salt and pepper to taste. Complete the basic recipe as written.

CLAM AND CORN SOUFFLÉ: Drain 1 eight-ounce can of minced clams; to the liquid, add milk to equal 1 cup; reserve it and the clams. In the butter for the *roux*, cook 1 medium onion, peeled and chopped fine, until it is translucent; make the *roux* with 5 tablespoonfuls of flour. Make the *béchamel* with the reserved liquid; add the clams and 1 ten-ounce package of frozen corn kernels, fully thawed to room temperature; season the mixture with a few drops of Tabasco sauce and salt to taste. Complete the basic recipe as written, using the yolks and whites of 5 eggs and baking the soufflé at 375° for 35 minutes.

COLLARD GREENS SOUFFLÉ: Follow the directions for Spinach Soufflé, page 14, using 1 ten-ounce package of frozen chopped collard greens, cooked until just tender according to the directions on the package, and pressed dry in a colander. Complete the basic recipe as written.

CREAMED CORN SOUFFLÉ: To the *roux*, add 1 small onion, peeled and grated, 2 powdered chicken bouillon cubes, a generous grating of nutmeg, and ¼ teaspoonful of white pepper. Make the *béchamel* with ½ cupful of milk (it will be very thick), and add to it 1 seventeen-ounce can of cream-style corn. Complete the basic recipe as written.

FENNEL SOUFFLÉ: Steam 2 large bulbs of fennel, rinsed and quartered, for 25 minutes or until the vegetable is tender; force it through a coarse sieve or purée it in the container of a food processor; reserve it. To the *roux*, add 2 powdered bouillon cubes. To the *béchamel*, add the fennel purée, ¼ cupful of fine-chopped parsley, and salt and pepper to taste. Complete the basic recipe as written.

FISH SOUFFLÉ: Crumb the buttered soufflé dish as described on page 5. To the *roux*, add 1 small onion, peeled and grated. To the *béchamel*, add 1 to 1½ cupfuls of cooked, boned, flaked white-fleshed fish of your choice (cod, flounder, halibut, scrod, sole, turbot), ¼ cupful of fine-chopped parsley, and salt and pepper to taste. Complete the basic recipe as written, using 5 egg whites.

FRESH CORN SOUFFLÉ: Cut the kernels from 5 large ears of uncooked corn; scrape the cobs to extract the milk (you should have about 2 cupfuls of corn); reserve it. To the *roux*, add 2 powdered bouillon cubes and a generous grating of nutmeg. Make the *béchamel* with ¾ cupful of milk (it will be quite thick); add the reserved corn and season the mixture with salt and white pepper to taste. Complete the basic recipe as written.

GREEN BEAN SOUFFLÉ: Cook, covered, ¾ pound fresh green beans, rinsed and trimmed, *or* 1 ten-ounce package frozen beans, in ½ cupful lightly salted water until they are tender (12 to 15 minutes); drain them, reserving the liquid. Chop the beans very fine or, if you prefer, purée them in the container of a food processor or blender; reserve them. To the bean liquid, add milk to equal 1 cup; reserve it. To the *roux*, add 1 small onion, peeled and grated, 2 powdered bouillon cubes, and ½ teaspoonful of ground coriander. Make the *béchamel* with the reserved liquid; to it, add the prepared beans and season the mixture with salt and pepper to taste. Complete the basic recipe as written.

GREEN ONION SOUFFLÉ: In the butter for the *roux*, cook 3 bunches (about 24) scallions, trimmed and chopped, with as much of the green part as is crisp; add 2 powdered bouillon cubes and the flour; over gentle heat, cook the mixture for a few minutes. Stir in the milk as directed, and to the *béchamel*, add 2 tablespoonfuls of grated Parmesan cheese and ¼ cupful of fine-chopped parsley; season the mixture with salt and pepper to taste. Complete the basic recipe as written.

GREEN PEA SOUFFLÉ: Use either 2 cupfuls of fresh peas, cooked until tender in lightly salted boiling water and drained, or 1 ten-ounce package of frozen tiny peas, fully thawed to room temperature (the frozen peas will not require cooking); the peas may be used whole *or* puréed. To the *roux*, add 1 small onion, peeled and grated, and 2 powdered bouillon cubes. To the *béchamel*, add the prepared peas, 3 tablespoonfuls of grated Parmesan cheese (optional), and salt and pepper to taste. Complete the basic recipe as written.

KALE SOUFFLÉ: Follow the directions for Spinach Soufflé, page 14, using 1 ten-ounce package of frozen chopped kale, cooked until just tender according to the directions on the package and pressed dry in a colander. Complete the basic recipe as written.

SOUFFLÉ LAURETTE: Follow the recipe for Cheese Soufflé, page 10. Using a rubber spatula, transfer one-half of the completed recipe to the prepared dish; over the batter, break 4 eggs, taking care that the yolks remain whole; cover them with the remaining batter. Complete the basic recipe as written. (If desired, you may add 4 eggs, in the same way, to Spinach Soufflé, page 14).

LETTUCE SOUFFLÉ: Use a variety of garden lettuces, rinsed, dried on absorbent paper, and chopped, to equal 2 cupfuls, tightly packed. In the butter for the *roux*, sauté the lettuce until it is limp; stir in the flour, 1 powdered bouillon cube, and 1 tablespoonful of grated onion. Add ⅔ cupful of milk to make the *béchamel*, stirring constantly until the mixture is thickened and smooth; season it with salt and white pepper to taste. Complete the basic recipe as written.

LIVER PÂTÉ SOUFFLÉ: In the butter for the *roux*, cook 1 medium onion, peeled and chopped fine, until it is translucent; complete the *roux* and *béchamel*. To the *béchamel*, add 2 four-ounce cans of liver pâté, whipped with a fork until light, and ⅓ cupful of fine-chopped parsley. Complete the basic recipe as written.

MUSTARD GREENS SOUFFLÉ: Follow the directions for Spinach Soufflé (below), using 1 ten-ounce package of frozen chopped mustard greens, cooked until just tender according to the directions on the package and pressed dry in a colander. Complete the basic recipe as written.

ONION SOUFFLÉ: Cook 6 medium onions, peeled and quartered, in lightly salted boiling water to cover, for 10 to 12 minutes, or until they are just tender. Drain them well; purée them in a blender or in the container of a food processor; reserve the purée. Prepare the *roux* as directed. Make the *béchamel* with ½ cupful of milk; to it, add the onion purée and season the mixture with salt and pepper to taste. Complete the basic recipe as written.

ROQUEFORT SOUFFLÉ: This recipe must be made with Roquefort cheese; blue cheese, which is oily, will not yield a well-puffed soufflé. To the hot *béchamel*, add 1½ cupfuls (6 ounces) crumbled Roquefort cheese, ½ teaspoonful salt, and ¼ teaspoon pepper; stir the mixture, *partially* melting the cheese. Complete the basic recipe as written.

SHAD ROE SOUFFLÉ: The soufflé may be made with any delicately flavored fish roe. Cover 1 pair medium shad roe with boiling, lightly salted water to which 2 tablespoonfuls of fresh lemon juice have been added; simmer the roe very gently, uncoverel, for 12 minutes. Drain and refresh them in cold water; pat them dry with absorbent paper; remove the membranes and, with a fork, gently separate the eggs. Reserve the roe. To the *roux*, add 1 powdered bouillon cube and 2 tablespoonfuls of onion, chopped very fine. Beat the egg yolks into the *béchamel* and season the mixture with salt and pepper to taste. Fold in the reserved shad roe. In order not to bruise the roe, fold in *all* of the egg white. Complete the basic recipe as written.

SPINACH SOUFFLÉ: Use 1 ten-ounce package of fresh spinach, the woody stems removed, rinsed, plunged into boiling salted water for 30 seconds, pressed dry in a colander, and chopped fine (*or* 1 ten-ounce package of frozen chopped spinach, fully thawed to room temperature and pressed dry in a colander). Reserve the prepared spinach. To the *roux*, add 2 powdered bouillon cubes. To the *béchamel*, add the reserved spinach and season the mixture with salt and pepper to taste. Complete the basic recipe as written.

SPINACH AND HAM SOUFFLÉ: Follow the directions for Spinach Soufflé (above), adding to the *béchamel* ½ cupful of cooked ham cut into fine dice; add the spinach and complete the basic recipe as written.

SUMMER SQUASH SOUFFLÉ: Rinse and trim 5 medium size yellow summer squash; chop them very coarse and steam them for 8 minutes, or until they are just tender. Purée them in the container of a food processor or blender; reserve the purée. To the *roux*, add 1 small onion, peeled and grated, and a generous grating of nutmeg. Omit the milk and make the *béchamel* with the reserved purée as the liquid ingredient. Complete the basic recipe as written.

SWEETBREAD SOUFFLÉ: In 1 quart of simmering water seasoned with 1 teaspoonful of salt and 2 tablespoonfuls of lemon juice, cook 1 pound (1 pair) of sweetbreads for 20 minutes. Refresh them in cold water; cover with cold water and refrigerate them until chilled; drain and remove the veins and membranes; chop them coarse and reserve. Using the prepared sweetbreads, follow the directions for Calf's Brains Soufflé, page 9.

SWEET PEPPER SOUFFLÉ: Remove the stems and seeds from 2 medium-size sweet green and 2 medium-size sweet red peppers (if red peppers are not available, use 4 green ones). Cut them into lengthwise pieces and remove the ribs; cut the strips into ½-inch dice. In boiling salted water, wilt the pepper dice, uncovered, for 2 minutes. Refresh them in cold water; drain on absorbent paper, and reserve them. To the *roux*, add 2 powdered bouillon cubes. To the *béchamel*, add 2 tablespoonfuls of grated Parmesan cheese (optional) and the reserved pepper dice; season the mixture with salt and pepper to taste. Complete the basic recipe as written.

TURKEY SOUFFLÉ: To the *roux*, add 2 powdered chicken bouillon cubes. To the *béchamel*, add 1 cup of fine-minced or ground cooked turkey meat and ¼ cupful of fine-chopped parsley. Complete the basic recipe as written.

WATERCRESS SOUFFLÉ: From 1 large bunch of watercress, discard the woody stems. Rinse the watercress, drain, and dry it on absorbent paper; chop it fine and reserve it. To the *roux*, add 1 small onion, peeled and grated. To the *béchamel*, add the reserved watercress, 2 teaspoonfuls of Worcestershire sauce, a few drops of Tabasco sauce, and salt to taste. Complete the basic recipe as written.

WINTER SQUASH SOUFFLÉ: In the butter for the *roux*, cook 1 small onion, peeled and chopped fine, until it is translucent; add a generous grating of nutmeg to the *roux*. Make the *béchamel* with ¾ cupful of milk and add to it 1½ cupfuls of cooked winter squash, mashed until smooth (*or* 1 ten-ounce package frozen mashed Hubbard Squash, fully thawed to room temperature), ¼ cupful of fine-chopped parsley, and salt and pepper to taste. Complete the basic recipe as written, baking the soufflé at 350° for 45 minutes, or until it is well-puffed and golden.

ZUCCHINI SOUFFLÉ: Into a colander, grate 4 medium-large zucchini, rinsed and the ends trimmed; toss the vegetable with 2 teaspoonfuls of salt, cover it with a heavy plate, and allow it to drain for one hour (collect the liquid—it is a fine soup stock). To the *roux*, add 2 powdered bouillon cubes. Make the *béchamel* with ¾ cupful of milk (it will be thick); stir in the drained zucchini and season the mixture with salt and pepper to taste. Complete the basic recipe as written.

## Anchovy Soufflé

4 SERVINGS
PREPARATION: 30 MINUTES
COOKING: 30 MINUTES IN A 350° OVEN

*All the ingredients may be readied ahead and combined according to the directions at the time of cooking.*

Thoroughly butter and crumb a 2-quart soufflé dish.

**3 two-ounce cans flat anchovy filets**

In a sieve over a small bowl, drain the anchovy filets, separating them with a fork to facilitate the draining. Transfer 4 tablespoonfuls of the oil to a large saucepan. Discard the remainder. Reserve the filets.

**Reserved anchovy filets**
**1 cup milk**

In the container of an electric blender, combine the anchovy filets and milk; whirl them until the mixture is smooth. Reserve it.

**4 tablespoons flour**

Heat the reserved oil and in it, over gentle heat, cook the flour for a few minutes. Gradually add the reserved anchovy-milk, stirring constantly until the mixture is thickened and smooth.

**4 egg yolks**
**½ cup fine-chopped parsley**
**2 teaspoons Worcestershire sauce**

To the contents of the saucepan, add the egg yolks, beating to blend the mixture well. Stir in the parsley and seasonings.

**5 egg whites, beaten until stiff but not dry**

Into the mixture, beat one-fifth of the egg white; fold in the remainder. Using a rubber spatula, transfer the mixture to the prepared dish. Bake the soufflé at 350° for 30 minutes, or until it is well-puffed and golden.

**Cucumber Sauce, page 187 (optional)**

Cucumber sauce is a pleasant complement to this soufflé; offer it separately.

*Variation:*

SARDINE SOUFFLÉ: Use 2 four-and-three-quarter-ounce cans boneless, skinless sardines in place of the anchovies; drain them and use the oil as indicated above; with the tines of a fork, mash the sardines until smooth. Add to the *roux* 1 small onion, peeled and grated. To the *béchamel*, add the sardines. Complete the recipe as written.

## Apple and Onion Soufflé

4 SERVINGS
PREPARATION: 35 MINUTES
COOKING: 35 MINUTES IN A 350° OVEN

*All the ingredients may be readied ahead and combined according to the directions at the time of cooking.*

Thoroughly butter and crumb a 2-quart soufflé dish.

> **4 tablespoons butter**
> **3 medium-size onions, peeled and chopped fine**
> **4 tablespoons flour**

In a saucepan, heat the butter and in it cook the onion until translucent. Stir in the flour and, over gentle heat, cook the mixture for a few minutes.

> **½ cup milk**
> **3 medium-size tart apples, peeled**
> **Salt**
> **White pepper**

Gradually add the milk, stirring constantly until the mixture is thickened and smooth. Into the *béchamel*, grate the apples, stirring the mixture well after the addition of each apple; season it with salt and pepper to taste.

> **4 egg yolks**

Beat in the egg yolks

> **4 egg whites, beaten until stiff but not dry**

Into the mixture, beat one-fifth of the egg white; fold in the remainder. Using a rubber spatula, transfer the batter to the prepared dish. Bake the soufflé at 350° for 35 minutes, or until it is well-puffed and golden.

# Cornmeal Soufflé (Spoon Bread)

4 TO 6 SERVINGS
PREPARATION: 35 MINUTES
COOKING: 40 MINUTES IN A 350° OVEN

*Spoon bread is best made and baked in one continuous procedure; measure out the ingredients, scald the milk and cream, separate the eggs; prepare the recipe only when you are ready to cook it.*

Thoroughly butter a 2-quart baking or soufflé dish.

> 2½ cups boiling water
> 1¼ teaspoons salt
> 1½ cups white *or* yellow cornmeal

Into the boiling water, stir the salt. Gradually add the cornmeal in a steady stream, stirring constantly until the mixture is smooth; cook it for 1 minute. Remove the saucepan from the heat and allow it to cool to lukewarm.

> 4 tablespoons butter, melted
> 1 cup light cream, plus ¾ cup milk, scalded and cooled to lukewarm
> 4 egg yolks

Into the cornmeal mixture, stir first the butter and then the cream. Beat in the egg yolks.

> 5 egg whites, beaten until stiff but not dry

Into the mixture, beat one-fifth of the egg white; fold in the remainder. Using a rubber spatula, transfer the batter to the prepared dish. Bake the spoon bread at 350° for 40 minutes, or until a sharp knife inserted comes out clean.

## Cornmeal Soufflé with Chicken

4 TO 6 SERVINGS
PREPARATION: 40 MINUTES
COOKING: 40 MINUTES IN A 350° OVEN

*All the ingredients may be readied ahead and combined according to the directions at the time of cooking.*

Thoroughly butter a 2-quart soufflé dish.

> **2 cups milk**
> **1 tablespoon butter**
> **⅓ cup yellow cornmeal**

In a saucepan, combine the milk, butter, and cornmeal. Bring the milk to the boil, stirring; reduce the heat and cook the cornmeal, stirring constantly, until it is very thick.

> **1 cup grated mild Cheddar cheese**

Away from the heat, add the cheese, stirring until it is melted.

> **1 cup ground cooked chicken**
> **Salt**
> **Pepper**

Into the contents of the saucepan, stir the chicken. Season the mixture with salt and pepper to taste.

> **4 egg yolks**

Beat in the egg yolks.

> **4 egg whites, beaten until stiff but not dry**

Into the mixture, beat one-fifth of the egg white; fold in the remainder. Using a rubber spatula, transfer the batter to the prepared dish. Bake the soufflé at 350° for 40 minutes, or until it is well-puffed and golden.

## Curried Eggplant Soufflé

4 SERVINGS

PREPARATION: 40 MINUTES (THE PREPARATION TIME DOES NOT INCLUDE
  COOKING THE EGGPLANT)

COOKING: 30 MINUTES IN A 350° OVEN

*All the ingredients may be readied ahead and combined according to
the directions at the time of cooking.*

Thoroughly butter a 2-quart soufflé dish.

**1 large or 2 small eggplant**

With the tines of a fork, pierce the eggplant in several places; bake it
at 400° for 30 minutes; quarter it lengthwise, scoop out the pulp, and
discard the skins. Reserve the pulp.

| | |
|---|---|
| **4 tablespoons flour** | **Strained juice and grated rind** |
| **Reserved eggplant pulp** | **of ½ medium-size lemon** |
| **4 egg yolks** | **1 teaspoon curry powder (or** |
| **1 clove garlic, put through** | **more, to taste)** |
| **a press** | **1 teaspoon salt** |
| | **½ teaspoon pepper** |

In a mixing bowl, combine the flour, eggplant pulp, egg yolks, garlic,
lemon juice and rind, curry powder, salt, and pepper. Using a rotary
beater, blend the mixture until it is smooth.

**4 egg whites, beaten until stiff but not dry**

Into the mixture, beat one-fifth of the egg white; fold in the remainder.
Using a rubber spatula, transfer the batter to the prepared dish. Bake
the soufflé at 350° for 30 minutes, or until it is well-puffed and golden.

## Fresh Herb Soufflé

4 SERVINGS
PREPARATION: 40 MINUTES
COOKING: 30 MINUTES IN A 350° OVEN

*A soufflé for herb growers. If you have all the herbs listed growing in your garden, use them all; or make a selection of those that appeal to you.*

*All the ingredients may be readied ahead and combined according to the directions at the time of cooking.*

Thoroughly butter a 2-quart soufflé dish.

- 4 tablespoons butter
- 6 scallions, trimmed and chopped, with some of the green
- 4 tablespoons flour

In a saucepan, heat the butter and in it cook the scallions until translucent. Stir in the flour and, over gentle heat, cook the mixture for a few minutes.

- 1 cup milk

Gradually add the milk, stirring constantly until the mixture is thickened and smooth.

- 4 large leaves basil ( or 2 teaspoons dried basil )
- 2 tablespoons chopped chives
- 3 sprigs marjoram, the leaves removed from the stems ( or 1 teaspoon dried marjoram )
- 3 sprigs oregano, the leaves removed from the stems ( or 1 teaspoon dried oregano )
- ½ cup parsley leaves
- 3 sprigs summer savory, the leaves removed from the stems ( or
- 1 teaspoon dried summer savory )
- 3 sprigs tarragon, the leaves removed from the stems ( or 1 teaspoon dried tarragon )
- 3 sprigs thyme, the leaves removed from the stems ( or ¾ teaspoon dried thyme )
- 1 bunch watercress, rinsed, dried, the lower stems discarded

In a large measuring cup, combine the herb leaves; with a pair of scissors, cut them fine. (If you use dried herbs, combine them in a mortar and grind them with a pestle.) Into the *béchamel*, stir the prepared herbs.

**4 egg yolks**
**Salt**
**Pepper**

Into the mixture, beat the egg yolks. Season with salt and pepper to taste.

**4 egg whites, beatten until stiff but not dry**

Beat in one-fifth of the egg whites; fold in the remainder. Using a rubber spatula, transfer the batter to the prepared dish. Bake the soufflé at 350° for 30 minutes, or until it is well-puffed and golden.


## Ground-Meat Soufflé

4 SERVINGS
PREPARATION: 30 MINUTES
COOKING: 35 MINUTES IN A 350° OVEN

*The ground meat should be the leanest possible.*

*All the ingredients may be readied ahead and combined according to the directions at the time of cooking.*

Thoroughly butter a 2-quart soufflé dish.

**4 tablespoons butter**
**3 tablespoons flour**
**1 small onion, peeled and grated**

In a saucepan, heat the butter and in it, over gentle heat, cook the flour for a few minutes. Stir in the grated onion.

**1 cup milk**
**½ cup bread crumbs**
**1 cup fine-ground cooked lean meat (beef, ham, lamb or veal)**

**2 teaspoons Worcestershire sauce**
**Salt**
**Pepper**

Gradually add the milk, stirring constantly until the mixture is thickened and smooth. Stir in first the bread crumbs and then the meat and Worcestershire sauce.* Season the mixture with salt and pepper to taste.

**4 egg yolks**

Into the mixture, beat the egg yolks.

**5 egg whites, beaten until stiff but not dry**

Beat one-fifth of the egg white; fold in the remainder. Using a rubber spatula, transfer the batter to the prepared dish. Bake the soufflé at 350° for 35 minutes, or until it is well-puffed and golden.

## Hominy Soufflé

4 SERVINGS

PREPARATION: 30 MINUTES (THE PREPARATION TIME DOES NOT INCLUDE
  COOKING THE GRITS)
COOKING: 30 MINUTES IN A 350° OVEN

*All the ingredients may be readied ahead and combined according to the directions at the time of cooking.*

Thoroughly butter a 2-quart soufflé dish.

**1 cup milk**
**1 cup water**
**½ cup hominy grits**

In the top of a double boiler, combine the milk, water, and hominy grits. Over simmering water, cook the mixture, stirring it occasionally, for 1 hour; while cooking, it should be tightly covered.

**3 tablespoons butter**
**¼ cup grated mild Cheddar cheese (optional)**
**¾ teaspoon salt**
**¼ teaspoon white pepper**

---

* If desired, ⅓ cup grated Cheddar cheese, mild or sharp, may be added with the ground meat.

Remove the top of the doubler boiler from the simmering water. Stir in the butter, cheese, and seasonings. Transfer the mixture to a bowl and allow it to cool.

**4 egg yolks**

Into the mixture, beat the egg yolks.

**4 or 5 egg whites, beaten until stiff but not dry**

Beat in one-fifth of the egg white; fold in the remainder. With a rubber spatula, transfer the batter to the prepared dish. Bake the soufflé at 350° for 30 minutes, or until it is well-puffed and golden.

## Mushroom Soufflé

4 SERVINGS
PREPARATION: 30 MINUTES
COOKING: 30 MINUTES IN A 350° OVEN

*All the ingredients may be readied ahead and combined according to the directions at the time of cooking.*

Thoroughly butter and crumb a 2-quart soufflé dish.

**½ pound mushrooms**

With a damp cloth, wipe the mushrooms clean and chop them medium-coarse. Reserve them.

**4 tablespoons butter**
**Reserved mushrooms**

In a saucepan, heat the butter and in it cook the mushrooms, stirring, until they are limp. Drain them, reserving both the mushrooms and the liquid.

**Milk**

To the mushroom liquid, add milk to equal 1 cup. Reserve it.

**4 tablespoons butter**
**4 tablespoons flour**
**Reserved milk mixture**
**Reserved mushrooms**

In the saucepan, heat the butter and in it, over gentle heat, cook the flour for a few minutes. Gradually add the milk mixture, stirring constantly until thickened and smooth. Stir in the mushrooms.

**4 egg yolks**
**¼ cup fine-chopped parsley**
**Salt**
**Pepper**

Into the mixture, beat the egg yolks; stir in the parsley. Season the batter to taste.

**4 egg whites, beaten until stiff but not dry**

Beat in one-fifth of the egg white; fold in the remainder. Using a rubber spatula, transfer the batter to the prepared dish. Bake the soufflé at 350° for 30 minutes, or until it is well-puffed and golden.

## Onion and Cheese Soufflé with Beer

4 SERVINGS
PREPARATION: 40 MINUTES
COOKING: 30 MINUTES IN A 350° OVEN

*All the ingredients may be readied ahead and combined according to the directions at the time of cooking.*

Thoroughly butter a 2-quart soufflé dish.

| | |
|---|---|
| **1 cup stale beer** | **½ teaspoon sugar** |
| **1 large onion, peeled and** | **1 teaspoon salt** |
| **chopped fine** | **¼ teaspoon white pepper** |
| **6 scallions, trimmed and** | |
| **chopped fine** | |

In a saucepan, combine the beer, onion, scallions, and seasonings. Bring the liquid to the boil, remove the pan from the heat, and allow it to stand, covered, while you make the *roux*.

**4 tablespoons butter**
**4 tablespoons flour**
**Grating of nutmeg**

In a saucepan, heat the butter and in it, over gentle heat, cook the flour for a few minutes. Stir in the nutmeg.

**Reserved beer mixture**

To the *roux*, gradually add the beer mixture, stirring constantly until the batter is thickened and smooth.

**⅓ cup grated Emmenthaler *or* Cheddar cheese**
**4 egg yolks**

Into the mixture, beat the cheese and then the egg yolks.

**4 egg whites, beaten until stiff but not dry**

Beat in one-fifth of the egg white; fold in the remainder. Using a rubber spatula, transfer the batter to the prepared dish. Bake the soufflé at 350° for 30 minutes, or until it is well-puffed and golden.


## Oyster Soufflé

4 SERVINGS
PREPARATION: 30 MINUTES
COOKING: 30 MINUTES IN A 350° OVEN

*All the ingredients may be readied ahead and combined according to the directions at the time of cooking.*

Thoroughly butter and crumb a 2-quart soufflé dish.

**1 pint shucked oysters**

In a saucepan, over gentle heat, cook the oysters in their liquid just until their edges barely curl. Drain them, reserving the liquid. If desired, purée the oysters by whirling them for 3 seconds in the container of an electric blender, *or* leave them whole; reserve the purée or whole oysters.

**4 tablespoons butter**
**5 tablespoons flour**

In a saucepan, heat the butter and in it, over gentle heat, cook the flour for a few minutes.

**Reserved oyster liquid**
**Light cream**

To the oyster liquid add cream to equal 1 cup. Gradually add this mixture to the *roux*, stirring constantly until the *béchamel* is thickened and smooth.

**Reserved oyster purée (if used)**
**½ cup fine-chopped parsley**
**Few drops of Tabasco sauce**
**Salt**

Into the *béchamel*, stir the oyster purée (if you are using whole oysters, continue to reserve them), the parsley, Tabasco sauce, and salt to taste.

**4 egg yolks**

Into the mixture, beat the egg yolks.

**4 egg whites, beaten until stiff but not dry**
**Reserved whole oysters (if used)**

Beat in one-fifth of the egg white; fold in the remainder. Using a rubber spatula, transfer one-half of the batter to the prepared dish. Over the batter, layer the reserved oysters; cover them with the remaining batter. Bake the soufflé at 350° for 30 minutes, or until it is well-puffed and golden.

## Potato Soufflé

4 SERVINGS
PREPARATION: 15 MINUTES (THE PREPARATION TIME DOES NOT INCLUDE
   READYING THE MASHED POTATO)
COOKING: 30 MINUTES IN A 350° OVEN

*All the ingredients may be readied ahead and combined according to the directions at the time of cooking.*

Thoroughly butter a 2-quart soufflé dish.

**2 cups seasoned mashed potato at room temperature**
**½ cup light cream**
**½ cup grated Swiss cheese**
**¼ cup fine-chopped parsley**

In a mixing bowl, combine the potato, cream, cheese, and parsley; blend the mixture well.

**4 egg yolks**

Into the mixture, beat the egg yolks.

**4 egg whites, beaten until stiff but not dry**

Beat in one-fifth of the egg white; fold in the remainder. Using a rubber spatula, transfer the batter to the prepared dish. Bake the soufflé at 350° for 30 minutes, or until it is well-puffed and golden.

*Variations:*

SWEET POTATO SOUFFLÉ: Follow the directions as given above, using 2 cupfuls of seasoned mashed potato; omit the cheese.

JERUSALEM ARTICHOKE SOUFFLÉ: In place of the mashed potato, use 2 cupfuls of seasoned mashed Jerusalem artichokes.

## Pumpkin Spoon Bread

4 TO 6 SERVINGS
PREPARATION: 35 MINUTES
COOKING: 45 MINUTES IN A 375° OVEN

*Spoon bread is best made and baked in one continuous procedure. Measure out the ingredients, separate the eggs; prepare the recipe only when you are ready to cook it.*

Thoroughly butter a 2-quart baking or soufflé dish.

**1½ cups milk**
**½ cup white *or* yellow cornmeal**

In a saucepan, bring the milk to the boil. In a steady stream, gradually add the cornmeal, stirring constantly. Cook the mixture for 1 minute; remove it from the heat.

1 cup canned pumpkin
  purée
3 tablespoons soft butter
2 tablespoons brown sugar

Generous grating of
  nutmeg
Salt
Pepper

Into the cornmeal stir the pumpkin purée, butter, brown sugar, and nutmeg; season the mixture with salt and pepper to taste.

4 egg yolks
1½ teaspoons baking powder

Into the mixture, beat the egg yolks and baking powder.

4 or 5 egg whites, beaten until stiff but not dry

Beat in one-fifth of the egg white; fold in the remainder. Using a rubber spatula, transfer the batter to the prepared dish. Bake the spoon bread at 375° for 45 minutes, or until a sharp knife inserted comes out clean.

## Soufflé Provençale

4 SERVINGS
PREPARATION: 45 MINUTES
COOKING: 35 MINUTES IN A 350° OVEN

*All the ingredients may be readied ahead and combined according to the directions at the time of cooking.*

Thoroughly butter a 2-quart soufflé dish.

2 medium-size onions, peeled
  and chopped
3 cloves garlic, peeled and
  chopped fine
4 medium-size ripe tomatoes,
  peeled, seeded, and
  chopped

1 teaspoon oregano
1 teaspoon sugar
1 teaspoon salt
½ teaspoon pepper
¼ cup fine olive oil

In a skillet, combine the onion, garlic, tomatoes, seasonings, and olive oil. Stir the mixture to blend it well and, over medium heat, cook it, stirring often, until it is of a paste-like consistency. Allow it to cool. Reserve it.

| 3 tablespoons butter | 2 tablespoons grated |
|---|---|
| 4 tablespoons flour | Parmesan cheese |
| 1 cup milk | ¼ cup fine-chopped |
| Reserved tomato mixture | parsley |

In a saucepan, heat the butter and in it, over gentle heat, cook the flour for a few minutes. Gradually add the milk, stirring constantly until the mixture is thickened and smooth. Stir in the tomato mixture, cheese, and parsley.

**4 egg yolks**

Into the mixture, beat the egg yolks.

**4 egg whites, beaten until stiff but not dry**

Beat in one-fifth of the egg white; fold in the remainder. Using a rubber spatula, transfer the batter to the prepared dish. Bake the soufflé at 350° for 35 minutes, or until it is well-puffed and golden.

## Salmon Soufflé

4 SERVINGS
PREPARATION: 30 MINUTES
COOKING: 30 MINUTES IN A 350° OVEN

*All the ingredients may be readied ahead and combined according to the directions at the time of cooking.*

Thoroughly butter and crumb a 2-quart soufflé dish.

**1 seven-and-three-quarter-ounce can salmon, drained (reserve the liquid) and mashed with a fork**
**Milk**

Combine the reserved liquid and milk to equal 1 cup; reserve it.

| Reserved salmon | 2 tablespoons strained |
|---|---|
| Reserved milk | lemon juice |
| 1 small onion, peeled and | ¾ teaspoon salt |
| chopped coarse | ¼ teaspoon white |
| | pepper |

In the container of a food processor or electric blender, combine the salmon, milk, onion, lemon juice, and seasonings. Whirl them until the mixture is smooth.

**4 tablespoons butter**
**4 tablespoons flour**

In a saucepan, heat the butter and in it, over gentle heat, cook the flour for a few minutes. To the *roux*, add the salmon mixture, stirring constantly until the batter is thickened and smooth.

**4 egg yolks**
**¼ cup fine-chopped parsley**

Into the mixture, beat the egg yolks and parsley.

**4 egg whites, beaten until stiff but not dry**

Beat in one-fifth of the egg white; fold in the remainder. Using a rubber spatula, transfer the batter to the prepared dish. Bake the soufflé at 350° for 30 minutes, or until it is well-puffed and golden.

*Variations:*

SALMON AND BROCCOLI SOUFFLÉ : Follow the recipe as written, adding before the addition of the egg yolks, 1 ten-ounce package frozen chopped broccoli, cooked according to the directions on the package and pressed dry in a colander.

TUNA SOUFFLÉ : Follow the recipe as written, using 1 seven-ounce can water-pack tuna and its liquid instead of the salmon.

## Scallop Soufflé

4 SERVINGS
PREPARATION: 30 MINUTES
COOKING: 30 MINUTES IN A 375° OVEN

*All the ingredients may be readied ahead and combined according to the directions at the time of cooking.*

Thoroughly butter and crumb a 2-quart soufflé dish.

½ pound sea scallops
1 cup milk

In the container of a food processor or blender, combine the scallops and milk; whirl them until the mixture is smooth. Reserve it.

4 tablespoons butter
1 medium-size onion, peeled and chopped fine
2 powdered bouillon cubes
¼ teaspoon white pepper
4 tablespoons flour

In a saucepan, heat the butter and in it cook the onion until translucent. Stir in the bouillon powder, pepper, and flour and, over gentle heat, cook the mixture for a few minutes.

**Reserved milk mixture**

Gradually add the milk mixture, stirring constantly until the batter is thickened and smooth.

4 egg yolks
⅓ cup fine-chopped parsley

Into the mixture, beat the egg yolks and parsley.

4 egg whites, beaten until stiff but not dry

Beat in one-fifth of the egg white; fold in the remainder. Using a rubber spatula, transfer the batter to the prepared dish. Bake the soufflé at 350° for 30 minutes, or until it is well-puffed and golden.

*Variations:*

CRAB OR LOBSTER SOUFFLÉ: Drain and reserve any liquid from 1 six-ounce can of crab or lobster meat; remove all pieces of tendon; combine the liquid and milk to equal 1 cup. In the container of a food processor or blender, combine the milk and crab or lobster meat; whirl them until the mixture is smooth. Prepare the *roux* as indicated; make the *béchamel* with the puréed mixture. Complete the recipe as written.

SHRIMP SOUFFLÉ (the preparation time is about 50 minutes): In ½ cupful of water, steam ¾ pound of raw, unshelled shrimp, stirring them often, until they are pink. Drain them, reserving the liquid; peel and chop very fine. Reserve them. To the liquid, add milk to equal 1 cup; reserve it. Make the *roux* and *béchamel* as indicated above, using the reserved milk as the liquid ingredient; to the *béchamel*, add the chopped shrimp. Complete the recipe as written.


## Tomato Soufflé

4 SERVINGS
PREPARATION: 25 MINUTES
COOKING: 30 MINUTES IN A 350° OVEN

*All the ingredients may be readied ahead and combined according to the directions at the time of cooking.*

Thoroughly butter and crumb a 2-quart soufflé dish.

> 3 tablespoons butter
> 3 tablespoons flour
> ¾ teaspoon salt
> ¼ teaspoon pepper

In a saucepan, heat the butter and in it, over gentle heat, cook the flour for a few minutes; stir in the seasonings.

> 1 six-ounce can tomato paste
> 1 large *or* 2 small ripe tomatoes, peeled, seeded, and chopped
>     with their liquid

To the *roux*, add the tomato paste and tomato, stirring constantly until the mixture is thickened and smooth.

> 4 egg yolks

Into the mixture, beat the egg yolks.

> 4 egg whites, beaten until stiff but not dry

Beat in one-fifth of the egg white; fold in the remainder. Using a rubber spatula, transfer the batter to the prepared dish. Bake the soufflé at 350° for 30 minutes, or until it is well-puffed and golden.

> Basil Sauce, page 187

Because tomatoes and basil complement each other so well, offer the sauce separately, if desired.

## Turnip Soufflé

4 SERVINGS
PREPARATION: 50 MINUTES
COOKING: 35 MINUTES IN A 375° OVEN

*All the ingredients may be readied ahead and combined according to the directions at the time of cooking.*

Thoroughly butter a 2-quart soufflé dish.

**4 or 5 medium white turnips, peeled and quartered**

In boiling salted water to cover, cook the turnips for 25 minutes, or until they are very tender. Drain and mash them until they are smooth, or purée them in the container of a food processor; reserve the purée.

**4 tablespoons butter**
**4 tablespoons flour**
**2 bouillon cubes, powdered**

In a saucepan, heat the butter and in it, over gentle heat, cook the flour for a few minutes; stir in the bouillon powder.

**¾ cup milk**
**Reserved turnip purée**
**Salt**
**Pepper**

To the *roux*, gradually add the milk, stirring constantly until the mixture is thickened and smooth; stir in the turnip and season the batter with salt and pepper to taste.

**4 egg yolks**

Into the mixture, beat the egg yolks.

**4 egg whites, beaten until stiff but not dry**

Beat in one-fifth of the egg white; fold in the remainder. Using a rubber spatula, transfer the batter to the prepared dish. Bake the soufflé at 375° for 35 minutes, or until it is well-puffed and golden.

*Variation:*

**PARSNIP SOUFFLÉ:** In place of the turnips, use ¾ pound parsnips, scraped, chopped coarse, and cooked in lightly salted boiling water for 40 minutes or until they are very tender. Drain and mash them until they are smooth, or purée them in the container of a food processor; reserve the purée. Complete the recipe as written.

## Mushroom Mousse: A Basic Recipe for Other Hot Vegetable Mousses

6 SERVINGS

PREPARATION: 30 MINUTES

COOKING: 40 MINUTES IN A 375° OVEN

*All the ingredients may be readied ahead and combined according to the directions at the time of cooking.*

Thoroughly butter a 6-cup ring mold.

> **1 pound mushrooms, wiped clean with a damp cloth and chopped fine**

Prepare the mushrooms.

> **2 tablespoons butter**
> **2 tablespoons flour**

In a saucepan, heat the butter and in it, over gentle heat, cook the flour for a few minutes. Add the prepared mushrooms and cook them, stirring for 2 minutes. Allow the mixture to cool.

> **3 egg yolks**
> **½ teaspoon curry powder, if desired**
> **½ teaspoon salt**
> **¼ teaspoon pepper**

Into the mushroom mixture, beat the egg yolks and the seasonings.

> **1 cup heavy cream, whipped**
> **3 egg whites, beaten until stiff but not dry**

Fold in the whipped cream. Beat in one-fifth of the egg white; fold in the remainder. Using a rubber spatula, transfer the batter to the prepared mold. Place the mold in a pan of hot water and bake the mousse at 375° for 40 minutes, or until it is well puffed. Allow it to stand for 5 minutes before unmolding it onto a heated serving dish.

For variation: In place of the mushrooms, use 1½ cupfuls of the following cooked vegetables, chopped fine or puréed:

ARTICHOKE HEARTS

GREEN BEANS

BROCCOLI

BRUSSELS SPROUTS

CARROTS

CELERY ROOT ( CELERIAC )

CORN

EGGPLANT

JERUSALEM ARTICHOKES

KOHLRABI

LIMA BEANS

PARSNIPS

PEAS

PUMPKIN

SPINACH

SUMMER SQUASH ( GRATED
COARSE AND DRAINED IN A
COLANDER FOR 1 HOUR )

TURNIPS

WINTER SQUASH

## Beet Mousse

6 SERVINGS

PREPARATION: 30 MINUTES (THE PREPARATION TIME DOES NOT INCLUDE
COOKING THE BEETS)

COOKING: 35 MINUTES IN A 350° OVEN

*All the ingredients may be readied ahead and combined according to
the directions at the time of cooking.*

Thoroughly butter a 5-cup ring mold.

**2 pounds fresh beets ( *or* 2 one-pound cans beets, drained and
puréed )**

In boiling salted water to cover, cook the beets for 45 minutes, or until
they are very tender. Skin and then chop them coarse. Purée them
in the container of a food processor or in a food mill. Reserve the
purée.

**3 tablespoons butter
1 large onion, peeled and chopped fine**

In a saucepan, heat the butter and in it, over gentle heat, cook the
onion until translucent.

**2 tablespoons plus 1 teaspoon flour
2 chicken bouillon cubes, dissolved in ½ cup hot water
½ cup light cream**

Into the onion stir the flour and allow it to cook for a few minutes; gradually add the bouillon and then the cream, stirring constantly until the mixture is thickened and smooth.

> **Reserved beet purée**
> **½ teaspoon nutmeg**
> **Salt**
> **Pepper**

Away from the heat, stir in the beet purée. Season the mixture with the nutmeg and salt and pepper to taste.

> **4 eggs**

Into the mixture, beat the eggs one at a time. Using a rubber spatula, transfer the batter to the prepared mold and place the mold in a pan of hot water. Bake the mousse at 350° for 35 minutes, or until a sharp knife inserted at the center comes out clean. Allow the mousse to stand for 5 minutes before unmolding it onto a heated plate.

> **Hollandaise Sauce, page 188**

Hollandaise sauce is delicious with this mousse; serve the sauce separately, if desired.


## Cauliflower Mousse

6 SERVINGS

PREPARATION: 40 MINUTES

COOKING: 45 MINUTES IN A 350° OVEN

*All the ingredients may be readied ahead and combined according to the directions at the time of cooking.*

*One-quarter of a pound of mushrooms, chopped fine and sautéed in butter, is a pleasant addition to this mousse. Drain the mushrooms and use the juice as part of the liquid measure. Add them along with the reserved cauliflower purée.*

Thoroughly butter a 5-cup ring mold.

1 one-pound head cauliflower

Remove the leaves and steam the cauliflower, whole, for 20 minutes, or until it is just tender; chop it coarse and, in the container of a food processor or food mill, purée it. Reserve the purée.

2 tablespoons butter
2 tablespoons flour
¾ cup milk

In a saucepan, heat the butter and in it, over gentle heat, cook the flour for a few minutes. Gradually add the milk, stirring constantly until the mixture is thickened and smooth.

Reserved cauliflower purée
3 eggs, lightly beaten
Worcestershire sauce
Salt
Pepper

Into the *béchamel*, stir the cauliflower purée and eggs; season the mixture to taste. Using a rubber spatula, transfer the batter to the prepared mold. Place the mold in a pan of hot water and bake the mousse at 350° for 45 minutes, or until a sharp knife inserted at the center comes out clean. Allow the mousse to stand for 5 minutes before unmolding it onto a heated serving plate.

## Chicken Mousse

6 SERVINGS
PREPARATION: 30 MINUTES (THE PREPARATION TIME DOES NOT INCLUDE
    COOKING THE CHICKEN, IF NECESSARY)
COOKING: 50 MINUTES IN A 350° OVEN

*This recipe is an attractive way to use leftover cooked chicken and may also be made with cooked turkey. One large full breast of chicken, simmered for 20 minutes in seasoned water, will yield the 1½ cupfuls of ground meat.*

*All the ingredients may be readied ahead and combined according to the directions at the time of cooking.*

Thoroughly butter a 5-cup ring mold.

> **4 tablespoons butter**
> **5 tablespoons flour**
> **1 cup milk**

In a saucepan, heat the butter and in it, over gentle heat, cook the flour for a few minutes. Gradually add the milk, stirring until the mixture is thickened and smooth.

> **3 egg yolks**
> **½ cup light cream**
> **1½ cups ground white meat of chicken**

In a mixing bowl, combine the egg yolks and cream; using a rotary beater, blend them well. Into the contents of the saucepan, stir the cream and then the chicken meat.

> **2 chicken bouillon cubes, powdered**
> **½ teaspoon white pepper**
> **Salt**

Stir in the bouillon powder and pepper; adjust the seasoning with additional salt, if necessary.

> **3 egg whites, beaten until stiff but not dry**

Into the mixture, beat in one-fifth of the egg white; fold in the remainder. Using a rubber spatula, transfer the mixture to the prepared mold and place the mold in a pan of hot water. Bake the mousse at 350° for 50 minutes, or until a sharp knife inserted at the center comes out clean. Allow the mousse to stand for 5 minutes before unmolding it onto a heated plate.

> **Mixed Vegetable Salad, page 197**

If desired, fill the center of the mousse with some of the vegetables; offer the remainder separately.

## Fish Mousse

6 SERVINGS
PREPARATION: 25 MINUTES
COOKING: 40 MINUTES IN A 350° OVEN

*This recipe may be made with any lean white-fleshed fish filet: cod, flounder, halibut, scrod, or sole.*

*All the ingredients may be readied ahead and combined according to the directions at the time of cooking.*

Thoroughly butter a 5-cup ring or other mold.

| | |
|---|---|
| 1 pound fish filets of your choice, chopped coarse | 1 teaspoon Worcestershire sauce |
| 1 small onion, peeled and chopped coarse | ¾ teaspoon salt |
| 1 tablespoon fresh lemon juice | ¼ teaspoon white pepper |

In the container of a food processor or blender, combine the fish, onion, lemon juice, and seasonings. Whirl them until the mixture is smooth. Transfer it to a mixing bowl.

1 cup heavy cream, whipped
3 egg whites, beaten until stiff but not dry

Fold in the whipped cream. Beat in one-fifth of the egg white, then fold in the remainder. Using a rubber spatula, transfer the mixture to the prepared mold and place the mold in a pan of hot water. Bake the mousse at 350° for 50 minutes, or until a sharp knife inserted at the center comes out clean. Allow the mousse to stand for 5 minutes before unmolding it onto a heated serving plate.

Hollandaise Sauce, page 188 (which you may prepare from the remaining egg yolks) *or* Green Mayonnaise, page 190

Offer the sauce of your choice separately.

## Liver Mousse

6 SERVINGS
PREPARATION: 25 MINUTES
COOKING: 1 HOUR IN A 325° OVEN

*This recipe may be made with chicken, calf, or beef liver.*

*All ingredients may be readied ahead and combined according to the directions at the time of cooking.*

Thoroughly butter a 5-cup ring mold or baking dish.

> 1 pound liver of your choice, chopped coarse
> 1 small onion, peeled and chopped coarse
> 1 cup milk
> 2 eggs
> 2 tablespoons potato starch

In the container of a food processor or electric blender, whirl the liver, onion, milk, eggs, and potato starch until the mixture is smooth.

> ¼ cup milk
> ¼ cup dry vermouth
> 2 bouillon cubes, powdered
> A few drops of Tabasco sauce

With the motor running, add the milk, vermouth, bouillon powder, and Tabasco sauce to the liver. Transfer the mixture to a mixing bowl.

> 1 five-and-one-third-ounce can unsweetened evaporated milk,
>     plus water to equal 1 cup

Stir in the evaporated milk. Pour the batter into the prepared utensil and set it in a pan of hot water. Bake the mousse at 325° for 1 hour, or until a sharp knife inserted at the center comes out clean. Allow the mousse to stand for 5 minutes before unmolding it onto a heated plate, or serve it directly from the baking dish.

Dill Sauce, page 188

Offer the dill sauce separately.

*Variation:*

**LAMB'S KIDNEY MOUSSE:** Prepare ¾ pound lamb's kidneys (remove the fat and soak them in cold salted water for at least one hour). Drain and dry the kidneys on absorbent paper. Using the prepared kidneys; follow the recipe for Liver Mousse (above).

## Meat Mousse

6 SERVINGS

PREPARATIONS: 30 MINUTES (THE PREPARATION TIME DOES NOT INCLUDE
   THE COOKING THE MEAT OF YOUR CHOICE)

COOKING: 50 MINUTES IN A 350° OVEN

*A recipe designed for leftover meats: beef, ham, lamb, pork, tongue, or veal. The meat should be very lean and ground very fine.*

*All the ingredients may be readied ahead and combined according to the directions at the time of cooking.*

Thoroughly butter a 5-cup ring mold.

> 4 tablespoons butter
> 5 tablespoons flour
> ¾ teaspoon dry mustard *or* ½ teaspoon nutmeg
> ¼ teaspoon pepper
> 1 cup milk

In a saucepan, heat the butter and in it, over gentle heat, cook the flour for a few minutes. Into the *roux*, stir the seasonings. Gradually add the milk, stirring constantly until the mixture is thickened and smooth.

> 3 egg yolks
> ½ cup light cream
> 1½ cups ground lean meat of your choice

In a mixing bowl, combine the egg yolks and cream; using a rotary beater, blend them well. Into the contents of the saucepan, stir the cream mixture and then the meat. Adjust the seasoning with salt to taste.

> 3 egg whites, beaten until stiff but not dry

Into the batter, beat one-fifth of the egg white, then fold in the remainder. Using a rubber spatula, transfer the mixture to the prepared mold and place the mold in a pan of hot water. Bake the mousse at 350° for 50 minutes, or until a sharp knife inserted at the center comes out clean. Allow the mousse to stand for 5 minutes before unmolding it onto a heated plate.

> Mixed Vegetable Salad, page 197

If desired, fill the center of the mousse with some of the vegetables; offer the remainder separately.

## Salmon Mousse

6 SERVINGS
PREPARATION: 45 MINUTES
COOKING: 40 MINUTES IN A 375° OVEN

*All the ingredients may be readied ahead and combined according to the directions at the time of cooking.*

Thoroughly butter a 6-cup ring mold.

> 1¼ pounds salmon steak ( *or* 2 seven-and-three-quarter-ounce
>     cans of salmon, drained, boned, and thoroughly mashed
>     with the tines of a fork )

If you are using fresh salmon, steam or poach it in very little water, until it flakes easily. Drain, skin, and bone it. With the tines of a fork, mash the fish until it is of a smooth consistency; or whirl it in the container of a food processor. Transfer it to a large mixing bowl.

> 1 small onion, peeled and grated
> Strained juice of 1 small lemon
> 1 teaspoon Worcestershire sauce ( optional )
> ¾ teaspoon salt
> ¼ teaspoon white pepper

To the fish, add the onion and seasonings, stirring to blend the mixture well.

> 3 egg whites

Into the fish mixture, beat the egg whites one at a time.

**1 cup heavy cream, whipped**

Fold in the whipped cream. Using a rubber spatula, transfer the batter to the prepared mold and place the mold in a pan of hot water. Bake the mousse at 375° for 40 minutes, or until a sharp knife inserted at the center comes out clean. Allow the mousse to stand for 5 minutes before unmolding it onto a heated plate.

**Hollandaise Sauce, page 188 or Mayonnaise-and-Lemon Sauce,
page 190 (make either sauce from the remaining egg yolks)**

Salmon mousse is particularly good with either of these sauces, which you may offer separately.

*Variations:*

**Tuna Mousse:** Follow the recipe as written, using, in place of the salmon, 1¼ pounds fresh tuna *or*, if desired, 2 seven-and-three-quarter-ounce cans water-pack tuna, well drained, the bones removed, and thoroughly mashed with the tines of a fork.

Or use any of the following instead of the salmon: cod, flounder, halibut, scrod, or sole.

## Spinach Mousse

4 TO 6 SERVINGS
PREPARATION: 30 MINUTES
COOKING: 30 MINUTES IN A 350° OVEN

*All the ingredients may be readied ahead and combined according to the direction at the time of cooking.*

Thoroughly butter a 6-cup ring mold.

**2 ten-ounce packages fresh spinach, the woody stems
removed, rinsed, wilted for 30 seconds in boiling water,
drained, and chopped; or 2 ten-ounce packages frozen
chopped spinach, fully thawed to room temperature and
pressed dry in a colander**

Prepare and reserve the spinach.

> **2 tablespoons butter**
> **2 tablespoons flour**
> **½ cup milk**

In a saucepan, heat the butter and in it, over gentle heat, cook the flour for a few minutes. Gradually add the milk, stirring constantly until the mixture is thickened and smooth.

> **Reserved spinach**
> **1 small onion, peeled and grated**
> **¾ teaspoon salt**
> **½ teaspoon pepper**

To the *béchamel*, add the spinach, onion, and seasonings; beat the mixture to blend it well.

> **4 egg whites, beaten until stiff but not dry**

Into the mixture, beat one-fifth of the egg white; fold in the remainder. Using a rubber spatula, transfer the batter to the prepared mold and place the mold in a pan of hot water. Bake the mousse at 350° for 30 minutes, or until a sharp knife inserted at the center comes out clean. Allow the mousse to stand for 5 minutes before unmolding it onto a heated plate.

> **Hollandaise Sauce, page 188**

Offer the Hollandaise sauce separately.

*Variations:*

**SPINACH MOUSSE WITH MUSHROOMS:** Increase the butter to 3 tablespoonfuls and in it sauté ¼ pound mushrooms, chopped fine; add the flour and complete the recipe as written.

**BROCCOLI MOUSSE:** Use 1 large bunch fresh broccoli or 2 ten-ounce packages frozen chopped broccoli; prepare the vegetable as indicated above (fresh broccoli will require 15 to 20 minutes cooking in one inch of boiling salted water). Proceed with the recipe as written.

# Cold Main-Dish Mousses

When unmolding a cold mousse, have its serving plate well chilled. Run a sharp-pointed knife around all edges of the mold. Into very warm, but not hot, water lower the mold to the level of the mousse and count to 8; remove the mold and quickly wipe away any excess water. Place the chilled serving plate, rinsed with cold water, over the mold; holding both mold and plate, invert and shake them gently. If this operation does not free the mousse onto the plate, set the dish on a firm surface and rap the mold sharply with your knuckles; two or three good thumps should be rewarded by the "squish" of the mousse as it settles comfortably onto its dish. Rinsing the serving plate in cold water will enable you to center the finished mousse so that it shows off to best advantage; before removing the mold, therefore, make sure that the mousse is positioned as you want it. Now lift the mold straight up from the mousse, set it aside, and return the quivering beauty to the refrigerator. A cold mousse may be unmolded two or three hours before serving. Take the mousse directly from refrigerator to table.

The time required to chill the gelatin mixture "until it just begins to set" varies for two reasons: the temperature of the mixture itself before the gelatin was added and the temperature of the added ingredient or ingredients (if chilled, the near-jelling time will be considerably reduced). After the gelatin mixture has reached room temperature and the chilled added ingredient(s) are added, allow about one hour for the mixture to "just begin to set."

## Avocado Mousse with Shrimp

6 SERVINGS
PREPARATION: 40 MINUTES
CHILLING TIME: 6 HOURS

Lightly oil and chill a 5-cup ring or other mold.

> 1 envelope unflavored gelatin, softened for 5 minutes in
> ¼ cup cold water

Over simmering water, dissolve the gelatin and reserve it.

> 2 large ripe avocados, peeled, seeded, and chopped coarse
> Strained juice of 1 medium-size lemon

In a mixing bowl, toss the avocado pieces with the lemon juice to pre-vent their discoloring. Reserve the mixture.

> Reserved gelatin
> Reserved avocado mixture
> ½ cup Mayonnaise, page 189
> ¾ teaspoon salt
> ½ teaspoon white pepper

In the container of a food processor or blender, combine the reserved gelatin and the avocado-lemon juice mixture; add to them the mayonnaise and seasonings. Whirl the mixture until it is smooth. Transfer the purée to a mixing bowl.

> 2 six-and-one-half-ounce cans small shrimp, rinsed under cold
> water and drained

Into the purée, fold the shrimp. Chill the mixture until it just begins to set.

> 1 cup heavy cream, whipped

Fold in the whipped cream. Using a rubber spatula, transfer the mixture to the prepared mold. Chill the mousse for at least 6 hours, or until it is thoroughly set.

> Mixed Vegetable Salad, page 197

Unmold the mousse onto a chilled serving plate. Fill the center with some of the salad and offer the remainder separately.

*Variation:*

If desired, you may omit the shrimp for Plain Avocado Mousse, which is very delicately flavored and especially good with Apple, Celery, and Green Pea Salad, page 193.

## Avocado Mousse with Watercress

6 SERVINGS
PREPARATION: 30 MINUTES
CHILLING TIME: 6 HOURS

*This dish may be made with either cream or cottage cheese; the choice is yours, depending upon the degree of richness you desire.*

Lightly oil and chill a 5- or 6-cup ring mold.

> 1 envelope unflavored gelatin, softened for 5 minutes in ¼
>     cup cold water

Over simmering water, dissolve the gelatin and reserve it.

> 2 large ripe avocados, peeled, seeded, and chopped coarse
> ½ cup fresh lime juice, strained

In a mixing bowl, toss the avocado pieces with the lime juice to prevent their discoloring. Reserve the mixture.

> Reserved gelatin
> Reserved avocado mixture
> 1 eight-ounce package cream cheese *or* 1 cup cottage cheese
> 1 cup cold milk
> ¾ teaspoon salt
> A few drops of Tabasco sauce

In the container of a food processor or blender, combine the reserved gelatin and avocado-lime juice mixture; add to them the cheese of your choice, the milk, and seasonings. Whirl the mixture until it is smooth. Transfer it to a mixing bowl.

> 1 bunch watercress, the woody stems removed, rinsed,
>     drained on absorbent paper, and chopped fine

Into the contents of the mixing bowl, fold the watercress. Using a rubber spatula, transfer the mixture to the prepared mold. Chill the mousse for at least 6 hours, or until it is thoroughly set.

**Chicken Salad, page 195**

Unmold the mousse onto a chilled serving plate. Fill the center with some of the salad and offer the remainder separately.

*Variations:*

ARTICHOKE MOUSSE: In place of the avocados and lime juice, use 2 nine-ounce packages frozen artichoke hearts, cooked in lightly salted water according to the directions on the package, and the strained juice of 1 large lemon. Thoroughly drain the artichokes and chop them coarse before putting them in the food processor. Omit the watercress. Complete the recipe as written.

BEET MOUSSE: In place of the avocados and lime juice, use 1 one-pound can shredded beets, drained, and the strained juice of 1 small lemon. Omit the watercress. Complete the recipe as written.

## Blue-Cheese Mousse

6 SERVINGS
PREPARATION: 30 MINUTES
CHILLING TIME: 6 HOURS

Lightly oil and chill a 5- or 6-cup ring mold.

> 1 envelope unflavored gelatin, softened for 5 minutes in
>    ½ cup cold water

Over simmering water, dissolve the gelatin and reserve it.

> 6 ounces blue cheese, at room temperature
> 3 ounces cream cheese, at room temperature
> Reserved gelatin

In a mixing bowl, using a rotary beater, whip the two cheeses until the mixture is light. Blend in the reserved gelatin.

1 two-ounce jar pimentos, drained and chopped fine
Salt
White pepper

Stir in the pimento. Season the mixture to taste. Chill it until it just begins to set.

1 cup heavy cream, whipped
2 egg whites, beaten until stiff but not dry

Fold in the whipped cream. Beat in a little of the egg white; fold in the remainder. Using a rubber spatula, transfer the mixture to the prepared mold. Chill the mousse for at least 6 hours, or until it is thoroughly set.

1 bunch watercress, the woody stems removed, rinsed, and
    thoroughly drained

Unmold the mousse onto a chilled serving plate and garnish it with watercress.

## Celeriac Mousse

6 SERVINGS
PREPARATION: 50 MINUTES
CHILLING TIME: 6 HOURS

Lightly oil and chill a 5- or 6-cup ring mold.

2 pounds celeriac (celery root), peeled and chopped coarse
Water
Salt

In a saucepan, combine the celeriac, water just to cover, and salt to taste. Bring the liquid to the boil, reduce the heat, and cook the celeriac, covered, for 20 minutes, or until it is tender. Drain it, reserving 1 cup of the water.

2 envelopes unflavored gelatin, softened for 5 minutes in
    ⅓ cup water

Over simmering water, dissolve the gelatin and reserve it.

Reserved celeriac and 1 cup celeriac water
Reserved gelatin
2 chicken bouillon cubes, powdered
½ teaspoon ground celery seed
½ teaspoon powdered cumin

In the container of a food processor or blender, combine the reserved celeriac and celeriac water, the gelatin, and the bouillon powder and seasonings. Whirl them until the mixture is smooth. Transfer to a mixing bowl and chill the mixture until it just begins to set.

1 cup heavy cream, whipped

Fold in the whipped cream. Using a rubber spatula, transfer the mixture to the prepared mold. Chill the mousse for at least 6 hours, or until it is thoroughly set. Unmold the mousse onto a chilled serving plate.

*Variations:*

**V ARIATION I :** To the contents of the food processor, add ½ cup mayonnaise; just before folding in the whipped cream, add 1 large tart apple, peeled, cored, and diced.

**V ARIATION II :** To the contents of the food processor, add 1 teaspoonful Dijon-style mustard; having transferred the mixture from the processor to the mixing bowl, stir in ½ pound shrimp, cooked, shelled, and diced, and 6 scallions, cut into thin rounds (the white part only).

## *Chicken Mousse—I*

6 SERVINGS
PREPARATION: 1 HOUR
CHILLING TIME: 6 HOURS

Lightly oil and chill a 5- or 6-cup ring mold.

1 pound boneless chicken breast, fat removed
2 cups water
1 bay leaf
Salt

In a saucepan, combine the chicken, water, bay leaf, and salt to taste. Bring the liquid to the boil, reduce the heat, and simmer the chicken, covered, for 20 minutes. Allow it to cool, covered, in the broth. Remove and dice it.

> 1½ envelopes unflavored gelatin, softened for 5 minutes in
>    ¼ cup cold water

Over simmering water, dissolve the gelatin and reserve it.

> ⅓ cup sherry
> ½ teaspoon paprika
> A few drops of Tabasco sauce
> Reserved chicken dice and broth
> Reserved gelatin

In the container of a food processor or blender, combine the sherry, paprika, Tabasco sauce, and the reserved chicken dice, broth, and gelatin. Whirl them until the mixture is smooth. Transfer it to a mixing bowl and chill until it just begins to set.

> ½ cup fine-chopped parsley
> 1 cup heavy cream, whipped

Stir in the parsley; fold in the whipped cream. Using a rubber spatula, transfer the mixture to the prepared mold. Chill the mousse for at least 6 hours, or until it is thoroughly set. Unmold it onto a chilled serving plate.

*Variation:*

**CHICKEN MOUSSE WITH ALMONDS:** Spread ½ cup slivered almonds on a baking sheet; toast them in a 350° oven for 10 to 15 minutes, or until they are a rich golden brown. Spread them on absorbent paper and crush them with a rolling pin. Stir the almonds into the mousse batter just before folding in the whipped cream.

## *Chicken Mousse—II*

6 SERVINGS

PREPARATION: 30 MINUTES (THE PREPARATION TIME DOES NOT INCLUDE
  COOKING THE CHICKEN)

CHILLING TIME: 6 HOURS

Lightly oil and chill a 5- or 6-cup ring mold.

> **1 envelope unflavored gelatin, softened for 5 minutes in ¼
>   cup cold water**

Over simmering water, dissolve the gelatin and reserve it.

> **1½ to 2 cups fine-chopped
>   cold cooked chicken
>   (see page 39), or you
>   may use leftover
>   chicken**
> **½ cup fine-chopped celery**
> **1 medium-size red onion,
>   chopped fine**
>
> **1½ cups Mayonnaise, page
>   189**
> **¼ cup tarragon-flavored
>   vinegar**
> **1 teaspoon salt**
> **A few drops of Tabasco
>   sauce**
> **Reserved gelatin**

If desired, put the chicken through the fine blade of a food grinder or
whirl it briefly in the container of a food processor. If the chicken is
diced or chopped very fine rather than puréed, the mousse will have an
interesting, rougher texture. In a mixing bowl, combine and blend the
chicken, celery, onion, mayonnaise, vinegar, seasonings, and gelatin.
Chill the mixture until it just begins to set.

> **1 cup heavy cream, whipped**

Fold in the whipped cream. Using a rubber spatula, transfer the mixture to the prepared mold. Chill the mousse for at least 6 hours, or
until it is thoroughly set.

> **Salad greens of your choice**
> **Dill Sauce, page 188**

Unmold the mousse onto a bed of salad greens and offer the sauce
separately.

*Variation:*

**Chicken Liver Mousse:** Use, in place of the chicken, 1 pound chicken livers, cooked until firm in lightly salted water to cover. Drain and allow them to cool. Chop the livers into fine dice or, if preferred, chop them coarse and then whirl them until smooth in the container of a food processor. Complete the recipe as written.

## Clam Mousse

6 SERVINGS

PREPARATION: 30 MINUTES

CHILLING TIME: 6 HOURS

Lightly oil and chill a 6-cup ring or other mold.

> **2 envelopes unflavored gelatin, softened for 5 minutes in ½ cup cold water**

Over simmering water, dissolve the gelatin and reserve it.

> **2 eight-ounce cans minced clams with their liquid**
> **1½ cups cream-style cottage cheese**
> **1 medium-size onion, peeled and chopped coarse**
> **Strained juice of 1 small lemon**

> **A few drops of Tabasco sauce**
> **1 teaspoon Worcestershire sauce**
> **1 teaspoon salt**

In the container of a food processor or blender, combine the clams, cottage cheese, onion, lemon juice, and seasonings. Whirl the mixture until it is smooth.

> **Reserved gelatin**
> **½ cup chopped parsley**

To the contents of the container, add the gelatin, whirling the mixture to blend it well. With the motor running, add the parsley and immediately turn off the motor. Transfer the mixture to a mixing bowl and chill it until it just begins to set.

1 cup heavy cream, whipped

Fold in the whipped cream. Using a rubber spatula, transfer the mixture to the prepared mold. Chill the mousse for at least 6 hours, or until it is thoroughly set.

1 bunch watercress, the woody stems removed, rinsed, and
    thoroughly drained

Unmold the mousse onto a chilled serving plate; garnish it with the watercress.

## Cucumber Mousse

6 SERVINGS

PREPARATION: 45 MINUTES (THE PREPARATION TIME DOES NOT INCLUDE
    DRAINING THE CUCUMBERS)

CHLLING TIME: 6 HOURS

Lightly oil and chill a 5-cup ring or other mold.

3 large cucumbers, peeled, halved lengthwise, seeded, and
    grated
2 teaspoons salt

In a mixing bowl, toss the cucumber with the salt. Transfer the vegetable to a colander, put a heavy plate on it, and allow it to drain for 45 minutes, reserving the liquid.

Reserved cucumber liquid plus water to equal 1 cup
2 envelopes unflavored gelatin

Sprinkle the gelatin over the liquid, allow it to soften for 5 minutes, and then dissolve it over simmering water. Reserve it.

2 cups cream-style cottage cheese
Reserved gelatin

In the container of a food processor or blender, combine the cottage cheese and gelatin; whirl them until the mixture is smooth. Transfer it to a mixing bowl.

Prepared cucumber
½ green pepper, seeded and
    chopped fine
4 scallions, trimmed and
    chopped fine, with as
    much of the green as is
    crisp

Strained juice and grated rind
    of 1 medium-size lemon
1 teaspoon sugar
A few drops of Tabasco
    sauce
A few drops of green food
    coloring (optional)

To the contents of the mixing bowl, add the cucumber, pepper, scallions, lemon juice, seasonings, and food coloring. Blend the mixture well and then chill it until it just begins to set.

**1 cup heavy cream, whipped**

Fold in the whipped cream. Using a rubber spatula, transfer the mixture to the prepared mold. Chill the mousse for at least 6 hours, or until it is thoroughly set.

**Salad greens of your choice**
**Bulgur Salad, page 194**

Unmold the mousse onto a bed of salad greens; fill the center with some of the salad and offer the remainder separately.

*Variation:*

**Asparagus Mousse:** Use, in place of the cucumbers, 1 pound fresh asparagus, trimmed, *or* 1 ten-ounce package frozen asparagus cuts, cooked in lightly salted water to cover for 15 minutes, or until the vegetable is very tender. Drain it, reserving 1 cup of the water. Soften the gelatin in ½ cup cold water and dissolve it in the asparagus water. Omit the green pepper and scallions. Complete the recipe as written.

## Green Pea Mousse

6 SERVINGS
PREPARATION: 40 MINUTES
CHILLING TIME: 6 HOURS

Lightly oil and chill a 5-cup ring or other mold.

1 envelope unflavored gelatin softened for 5 minutes in ¼
    cup cold water
1½ cups fresh peas *or* 1 ten-ounce package frozen peas
Water
Salt

In a saucepan, combine the peas, water just to cover, and salt to taste. Bring the liquid to the boil, reduce the heat somewhat, and cook the peas, covered, for 15 minutes, or until they are tender. Drain them and reserve both peas and liquid.

Reserved gelatin
Reserved pea liquid plus hot water, if necessary, to equal
    1 cup

Dissolve the gelatin in the hot liquid. Reserve it.

Reserved peas
1 cup sour cream *or* cream-style cottage cheese
¾ teaspoon salt
½ teaspoon white pepper
Reserved gelatin water

In the container of a food processor or blender, combine the peas, sour cream, seasonings, and gelatin. Whirl them until the mixture is smooth. Transfer it to a mixing bowl.

6 scallions, trimmed and chopped fine, with as much of the
    green as is crisp

Into the mixture, stir the scallions. Chill it until it just begins to set.

4 egg whites, beaten until stiff but not dry

Beat in one-fifth of the egg whites; fold in the remainder. Using a rubber spatula, transfer the mixture to the prepared mold. Chill the mousse for at least 6 hours, or until it is thoroughly set.

Watercress, the woody stems removed, rinsed, and
    thoroughly drained

Unmold the mousse onto a chilled serving plate and garnish it with watercress.

*Variation:*

**LIMA BEAN MOUSSE:** Use, in place of the peas, the same quantity of fresh or frozen lima beans; the cooking time will be a little longer. Complete the recipe as written.

## Ham Mousse

6 SERVINGS
PREPARATION: 30 MINUTES
CHILLING TIME: 6 HOURS

*A tasty way to use leftover ham.*

Lightly oil and chill a 6-cup ring or other mold.

> 1½ envelopes unflavored gelatin, softened for 5 minutes in
> ½ cup cold water

Over simmering water, dissolve the gelatin and reserve it.

> 3 cups fine-ground cooked lean ham
> 1½ teaspoons Dijon-style mustard
> 1½ teaspoons horseradish
> Reserved gelatin

In a mixing bowl, combine the ham, seasonings, and gelatin. Chill the mixture until it just begins to set.

> 1 cup heavy cream, whipped
> 3 egg whites, beaten until stiff but not dry

Fold in the whipped cream. Beat in one-fifth of the egg white; fold in the remainder. Using a rubber spatula, transfer the mixture to the prepared mold. Chill the mousse for at least 6 hours, or until it is thoroughly set. Unmold it onto a chilled serving plate.

*Variations:*

**CHICKEN MOUSSE:** Use, in place of the ham, an equal quantity of fine-ground cooked chicken; use the mustard and horseradish to taste, and adjust the seasoning with salt. Other recipes for cold chicken mousses appear on pages 52 and 54.

TONGUE MOUSSE: Use, in place of the ham, an equal amount of lean fine-ground cooked tongue. Complete the recipe as written.

## Horseradish Mousse

6 SERVINGS
PREPARATION: 35 MINUTES
CHILLING TIME: 6 HOURS

Lightly oil and chill a 5-cup ring or other mold.

> 1½ envelopes unflavored gelatin, softened for 5 minutes in
> ¾ cup water

Over simmering water, dissolve the gelatin and reserve it.

> 2 cups cream-style cottage cheese
> Reserved gelatin

In the container of a food processor or blender, combine the cottage cheese and reserved gelatin. Whirl the mixture until it is smooth. Transfer it to a mixing bowl.

> ½ cup prepared horseradish          1½ teaspoons sugar
> 1 medium clove garlic, put          ½ teaspoon salt
>    through a press                  A few drops green food
> ½ cup fine-chopped parsley             coloring (optional)

To the contents of the mixing bowl, add the horseradish, garlic, parsley, sugar, salt, and food coloring. Blend the mixture well and then chill it until it just begins to set.

> 1 cup heavy cream, whipped

Fold in the whipped cream. Using a rubber spatula, transfer the mixture to the prepared mold. Chill the mousse for at least 6 hours, or until it is thoroughly set.

**Chicken Salad, page 195**

Unmold the mousse onto a chilled serving plate. Fill the center with some of the chicken salad and offer the rest separately.

*Variation:*

**APPLE AND HORSERADISH MOUSSE:** Add to the contents of the mixing bowl, 1 large tart apple, peeled and grated; if desired, increase the sugar to 1 tablespoonful.

## Saffron Rice Mousse

6 SERVINGS
PREPARATION: 45 MINUTES
CHILLING TIME: 6 HOURS

Lightly oil and chill a 6-cup ring or other mold.

> 1½ envelopes unflavored gelatin, softened for 5 minutes in
> ½ cup cold water

Over simmering water, dissolve the gelatin and reserve it.

> 1 cup raw natural rice, cooked, covered in 2 cups lightly
>   salted water for 15 minutes, or until the liquid is
>   absorbed and the rice is tender
> ¼ teaspoon saffron, crumbled

To the rice, add the saffron; using two forks, toss the rice until it is light and fluffy. Reserve it.

> 1½ cups milk
> 1 small onion, peeled and
>   grated
> ¼ cup fine-chopped parsley
>
> A few drops Tabasco
>   sauce
> Reserved gelatin
> Reserved rice
> Salt

In a mixing bowl, combine the milk, onion, parsley, Tabasco sauce, and reserved gelatin and rice. Blend the mixture well; adjust the seasoning, to taste. Chill until it just begins to set. Stir it well to bring the rice from the bottom.

> 1 cup heavy cream, whipped

Fold in the whipped cream. Using a rubber spatula, transfer the mixture to the prepared mold. Chill the mousse for at least 6 hours, or until it is thoroughly set.

**Mixed Vegetable Salad, page 197**

Unmold the mousse onto a chilled serving plate. Fill the center with some of the salad and offer the remainder separately.

*Variation:*

CHEDDAR CHEESE MOUSSE : Use, in place of the rice and saffron, 1½ cupfuls of mild or sharp Cheddar cheese, grated fine. Complete the recipe as written.

## Salmon Mousse

6 SERVINGS
PREPARATION: 30 MINUTES
CHILLING TIME: 6 HOURS

Lightly oil and chill a 6-cup ring or other mold.

> 1 envelope plus 1 teaspoon unflavored gelatin softened for
>    5 minutes in ½ cup cold water
> ½ cup boiling water

To the softened gelatin, add the boiling water, stirring until the gelatin is dissolved. Reserve it.

| | |
|---|---|
| **Reserved gelatin** | **Strained juice of 1** |
| **2 seven-and-three-quarter-** | **medium-size lemon** |
| **ounce cans salmon,** | **½ teaspoon paprika** |
| **drained, the skin and** | **A few drops of Tabasco** |
| **bones removed** | **sauce** |
| **1 small onion, peeled and** | **2 teaspoons Worcester-** |
| **chopped coarse** | **shire sauce** |
| | **1 teaspoon salt** |

In the container of a food processor or electric blender, combine the gelatin, salmon, onion, lemon juice, and seasonings. Whirl them until the mixture is smooth. Transfer it to a mixing bowl.

⅔ cup Mayonnaise, page 189
2 cups cream-style cottage cheese, sieved or whirled in a food
    processor or blender until smooth

To the contents of the mixing bowl, add the mayonnaise and cottage cheese. Blend the mixture well and then chill it until it just begins to set.

1 cup heavy cream, whipped

Fold in the whipped cream. Using a rubber spatula, transfer the mixture to the prepared mold. Chill the mousse for at least 6 hours, or until it is thoroughly set. Unmold the mousse onto a chilled serving plate.

*Variations:*

SALMON ROE MOUSSE: Use, in place of the salmon, 2 three-and-one-third-ounce jars of salmon caviar, folded in just before the addition of the whipped cream; omit the salt.

TUNA MOUSSE: Use, in place of the salmon, the same quantity of water-pack tuna, well drained. If desired, add to the contents of the processor ¾ teaspoonful of curry powder.

LIVER PÂTÉ MOUSSE: Use, in place of the salmon, 3 four-ounce cans of liver pâté. Omit the mayonnaise.

## *Shrimp Mousse*

6 SERVINGS
PREPARATION: 25 MINUTES
CHILLING TIME: 6 HOURS

Lightly oil and chill a 5-cup ring or other mold.

1½ envelopes unflavored gelatin softened for 5 minutes in
    ½ cup cold water

Over simmering water, dissolve the gelatin and reserve it.

2 four-and-one-half-ounce cans small shrimp, with their liquid

1 small onion, peeled and chopped coarse

2 cups cream-style cottage cheese

Strained juice and grated rind of 1 medium-size lemon

Reserved gelatin

In the container of a food processor or blender, combine the shrimp, onion, cottage cheese, lemon juice and rind, and gelatin. Whirl them until the mixture is smooth. Transfer it to a mixing bowl.

½ cup fine-chopped parsley
A few drops of Tabasco sauce
Worcestershire sauce (optional)
Salt

Stir in the parsley and adjust the seasoning to taste. Chill the mixture until it just begins to set.

4 egg whites, beaten until stiff but not dry

Using a rotary beater, whip the mixture to make it as light as possible. Beat in one-fifth of the egg white; fold in the remainder. Using a rubber spatula, transfer the mixture to the prepared mold. Chill the mousse for at least 6 hours, or until it is thoroughly set.

Mixed Vegetable Salad, page 197

Unmold the mousse onto a chilled serving plate. Fill the center with some of the salad and offer the remainder separately.


## Spinach Mousse

6 SERVINGS
PREPARATION: 40 MINUTES
CHILLING TIME: 6 HOURS

Lightly oil and chill a 5-cup ring or other mold.

2 envelopes unflavored gelatin, softened for 5 minutes in ½ cup cold water

Over simmering water, dissolve the gelatin and reserve it.

2 ten-ounce packages fresh spinach, the woody stems removed, rinsed, wilted in boiling salted water for 30 seconds, thoroughly drained, and chopped, *or* 2 ten-ounce packages frozen chopped spinach, fully thawed to room temperature and pressed dry in a colander

1 medium-size onion, peeled and grated

In a mixing bowl, combine the spinach and onion.

2 cups cream-style cottage cheese

Strained juice and grated rind of 1 medium-size lemon

Fine-chopped fresh herb of your choice ( marjoram, oregano, summer savory are especially good )

Salt

½ teaspoon pepper

Reserved gelatin

In the container of a food processor or blender, whirl the cottage cheese until it is smooth and add it to the spinach; or sieve it directly into the mixing bowl. Combine the contents of the mixing bowl with the lemon juice and rind, fresh herb, and seasonings. Stir in the reserved gelatin. Chill the mixture until it just begins to set.

4 egg whites, beaten until stiff but not dry

Beat in one-fifth of the egg white; fold in the remainder. Using a rubber spatula, transfer the mixture to the prepared mold. Chill the mousse for at least 6 hours, or until it is thoroughly set.

Apple, Celery, and Green Pea Salad, page 193

Unmold the mousse onto a chilled serving plate. Fill the center with some of the salad and offer the remainder separately.

*Variations:*

Use, in place of the cottage cheese, 2 cupfuls of plain yogurt and, in place of the suggested herbs, 2 tablespoonfuls of fine-chopped fresh mint.

MIXED VEGETABLE MOUSSE: Use, in place of the spinach, 2 ten-ounce packages of frozen mixed vegetables, cooked according to the directions on the package and drained. Add the vegetables to the contents of the mixing bowl. Complete the recipe as written.

## Sweetbread Mousse

6 SERVINGS

PREPARATION: 30 MINUTES (THE PREPARATION TIME DOES NOT INCLUDE
READYING THE SWEETBREADS)

Lightly oil and chill a 5-cup ring or other mold.

**1 pound sweetbreads**

Prepare the sweetbreads as directed on page 15 and reserve them.

**1 envelope unflavored gelatin, softened for 5 minutes in
½ cup cold water**

Over simmering water, dissolve the gelatin and reserve it.

| | |
|---|---|
| **⅓ cup fine-chopped celery** | **Strained juice of ½** |
| **1 tablespoon grated onion** | **medium-size lemon** |
| **1 tablespoon fine-chopped** | **Reserved sweetbreads** |
| **green pepper** | **Reserved gelatin** |
| **¼ cup fine-chopped parsley** | **Salt** |

In a mixing bowl, combine the celery, onion, pepper, parsley, lemon
juice, sweetbreads, and gelatin. Stir the mixture to blend it well. Adjust
the seasoning to taste. Chill the mixture until it just begins to set.

**1 cup heavy cream, whipped**

Fold in the whipped cream. Using a rubber spatula, transfer the mixture
to the prepared mold. Chill the mousse for at least 6 hours, or until it
is thoroughly set.

**Bulgur Salad, page 194**

Unmold the mousse onto a chilled serving plate. Fill the center with
some of the salad and offer the remainder separately.

## Waldorf Salad Mousse

6 TO 8 SERVINGS

PREPARATION: 35 MINUTES

CHILLING TIME: 6 HOURS

Lightly oil and chill a 6-cup ring or other mold.

2 envelopes unflavored gelatin, softened for 5 minutes in
   ½ cup cold water

Over simmering water, dissolve the gelatin and reserve it.

3 large tart apples, peeled, cored, and diced
2 tablespoons strained lemon juice

In a mixing bowl, toss the apple with the lemon juice to prevent its discoloring.

3 medium-size ribs celery, diced
¾ cup chopped walnuts
Mayonnaise, page 189
Reserved gelatin

To the apple, add the celery and walnuts. Blend in just sufficient mayonnaise to bind the mixture. Stir in the gelatin. Chill the mixture until it just begins to set.

1 cup heavy cream, whipped
3 egg whites, beaten until stiff but not dry

Fold in the whipped cream. Beat in one-fifth of the egg white; fold in the remainder. Using a rubber spatula, transfer the mixture to the prepared mold. Chill the mousse for at least 6 hours, or until it is thoroughly set. Unmold it onto a chilled serving plate.

# Hot Dessert Soufflés

## Basic Recipe for Hot Dessert Soufflés
## (Béchamel or Cream Base)

6 SERVINGS

PREPARATION: 30 MINUTES (THE PREPARATION TIME WILL VARY DEPEND-
ING UPON HOW MUCH READYING THE MAIN INGREDIENT REQUIRES)

COOKING: FOR A FIRM SOUFFLÉ, 30 MINUTES IN A 350° OVEN; FOR A
CREAMY SOUFFLÉ, à la française, 20 TO 25 MINUTES IN A 375° OVEN.

*All the ingredients may be readied ahead and combined according to
the directions at the time of cooking.*

Thoroughly butter and sugar a 2-quart soufflé dish or, if you prefer, individual soufflé dishes. (Individual soufflés are usually baked at 400°
for 10 to 12 minutes.)

> 3 tablespoons butter
> 3 tablespoons flour

In a saucepan, heat the butter and in it, over gentle heat, cook the
flour for a few minutes. This mixture is called a *roux*.

### Special seasonings

If the recipe calls for such special seasonings as ground spices (for
example ginger, mace, nutmeg), add them to the *roux*; the butter in
the *roux* will facilitate eliminating small lumps, which you will not
want in the completed soufflé.

68

**1 cup milk**

Gradually add the milk, stirring constantly until the mixture is thickened and smooth. This mixture is called a *béchamel*.

**½ cup sugar**
**A pinch of salt**

Away from the heat, add the sugar and salt, stirring until they are dissolved. (You may use more or less sugar, to taste; ½ cup seems right for most hot dessert soufflés.)

**Prepared major ingredient**

Into the contents of the saucepan, blend the major ingredient (see individual recipes below).

**4 egg yolks**
**Liquid seasoning, if called for**

Beat in the egg yolks and liquid seasoning (vanilla or almond extract, etc.).

**4 egg whites, beaten until stiff but not dry, page 6**

Beat in one-fifth of the egg white; fold in the remainder. Using a rubber spatula, transfer the mixture to the prepared dish. Bake the soufflé according to the directions given above, or until it is well-puffed and golden.

ALMOND SOUFFLÉ: On a baking sheet, evenly spread 1 three-and-one-half ounce package of blanched slivered almonds; toast them in a 350° oven for 10 to 15 minutes, or until they are a deep golden brown. In the container of a food processor or electric blender, whirl them until they are ground fine. Reserve them. Increase the sugar to ⅔ cupful and, after it is dissolved, stir in the reserved almond "flour." Add, with the egg yolks, 1 teaspoonful of almond extract. Complete the basic recipe as written and bake the soufflé at 375° for 30 minutes, or until it is well-puffed and golden.

APRICOT SOUFFLÉ: Make the *béchamel* with ½ cupful of milk (it will be very thick); increase the sugar to ⅔ cupful. After dissolving the sugar, stir in 1¼ cupfuls of apricot purée (page 96) and the strained juice of ½ medium-size lemon; add, with the egg yolks, ¼ teaspoonful of almond extract. Complete the basic recipe as written.

BANANA SOUFFLÉ: Into the *roux*, stir ¼ teaspoonful of mace; make the *béchamel* with ¾ cupful milk; into the *béchamel*, stir ¼ cupful of cognac. After dissolving the sugar, stir in 2 large *very* ripe bananas, peeled and puréed. Complete the basic recipe as written.

CHERRY SOUFFLÉ: To make the *béchamel*, use the liquid from 1 one-pound can of dark sweet pitted cherries plus milk to equal 1 cupful; add, with the egg yolks, ¼ teaspoonful of almond extract; stir in the reserved cherries, well drained and chopped coarse. Complete the basic recipe as written.

CHOCOLATE SOUFFLÉ: Reduce the sugar to ⅓ cupful and add with it 1 six-ounce package of semisweet chocolate bits; make sure that the chocolate is completely melted and that the mixture is smooth before continuing. Add, with the egg yolks, 1 teaspoonful of vanilla extract. Complete the basic recipe as written.

COFFEE SOUFFLÉ: After dissolving the sugar, stir in 2 table-spoonfuls of instant coffee powder of your choice. Complete the basic recipe as written.

DATE SOUFFLÉ: In 1 cupful of milk, cook ¾ cupful of fine-chopped pitted dates, covered, for 20 minutes, or until they are tender; drain and reserve them. To the cooking milk, add more milk, if necessary, to equal 1 cupful. To the *roux*, add a grating of nutmeg. Make the *béchamel* with the reserved milk; to it, add the reserved dates. Complete the basic recipe as written.

GINGER SOUFFLÉ: This soufflé, one of my favorites, may be made in two ways, both equally good.

I. To the *roux*, add 1 teaspoonful of powdered ginger. To the *béchamel*, add 2 tablespoonfuls of cognac. After dissolving the sugar, stir in ½ cupful of crystallized ginger, chopped fine. Complete the basic recipe as written.

II. Make the *béchamel* with ¾ cupful of milk; add to it ¼ cupful of cognac. Omit the sugar; stir into the *béchamel* 1 twelve-ounce jar of ginger marmalade. Complete the basic recipe as written and bake the soufflé at 350° for 40 minutes, or until it is well-puffed and golden.

**GRAND MARNIER SOUFFLÉ**: Make the *roux* with 4 table-spoonfuls of flour; reduce the sugar to ⅓ cupful; after dissolving it, stir in the grated rinds of 1 lemon and 1 orange, 2 tablespoonfuls of strained fresh lemon juice, and ⅓ cupful of Grand Marnier (or other orange-flavored liqueur). Use 5 egg whites. Complete the basic recipe as written.

**GRAND MARNIER SOUFFLÉ WITH ORANGE MAR-MALADE**: Make the *béchamel* with ¾ cupful of milk; reduce the sugar to ¼ cupful and, after dissolving it, stir in 4 tablespoonfuls of sweet orange marmalade and ½ cupful of Grand Marnier (or other orange-flavored liqueur). Complete the basic recipe as written and bake the soufflé at 375° for 35 minutes, or until it is well-puffed and golden.

**GUAVA SOUFFLÉ**: In the container of a food processor or electric blender, purée the drained guava shells from 1 fifteen-ounce can (available at specialty food stores); reserve the purée. Make the *roux* with 4 tablespoonfuls of butter and 4 tablespoonfuls of flour; into the *roux*, stir ½ teaspoonful of mace; reduce the sugar to ⅓ cupful and, after dissolving it, stir in the reserved guava purée. Use 5 egg whites. Complete the basic recipe as written and bake the soufflé at 375° for 30 minutes, or until it is well-puffed and golden.

**HAZELNUT SOUFFLÉ**: To the *béchamel*, add ¾ cupful of hazelnuts, crushed fine. Add, with the egg yolks, 1 teaspoonful of vanilla extract. Complete the basic recipe as written.

**KUMQUAT SOUFFLÉ** (the preparation time does not include readying the kumquat purée, page 197): Make the *roux* with 4 table-spoonfuls of butter and 4 tablespoonfuls of flour. Make the *béchamel* with ¾ cupful of milk; reduce the sugar to ¼ cupful and, after dissolving it, stir in 1 cupful of kumquat purée. Add, with the egg yolks, 1 teaspoonful of vanilla extract. Use 5 egg whites. Complete the basic recipe as written and bake the soufflé at 375° for 30 minutes, or until it is well-puffed and golden.

**LEMON SOUFFLÉ**: Increase the sugar to ¾ cupful and, after dissolving it, add the grated rind and strained juice of 1 large or 2 medium-size lemons. Complete the basic recipe as written.

LIME SOUFFLÉ: Increase the sugar to ¾ cupful and, after dissolving it, add the grated rind of 1 large lime and the strained juice of 2 limes. Complete the basic recipe as written.

MINCEMEAT SOUFFLÉ: Make the *béchamel* with ¾ cupful of milk; reduce the sugar to ¼ cupful and, after dissolving it, stir in 1 cupful of prepared commercial mincemeat and 2 tablespoonfuls of cognac. Add, with the egg yolks, 1 teaspoonful of vanilla extract. Complete the basic recipe as written and bake the soufflé at 375° for 30 minutes, or until it is well-puffed and golden.

ORANGE SOUFFLÉ: For the *béchamel*, use 1 six-ounce can frozen orange juice concentrate, fully thawed to room temperature, plus milk to equal 1 cupful; add, with the egg yolks, the grated rind of 1 large orange. Complete the basic recipe as written.

PRUNE SOUFFLÉ: Drain and remove the pits from 1 sixteen-ounce jar of cooked prunes; in the container of a food processor or electric blender, reduce the prunes to a smooth purée (you should have 1 cupful); reserve it. Make the *béchamel* with ¾ cupful of milk; reduce the sugar to ¼ cupful and, after dissolving it, stir in the reserved prune purée. Add, with the egg yolks, 1 teaspoonful of vanilla extract. Complete the basic recipe as written.

PUMPKIN SOUFFLÉ: After dissolving the sugar, add 1 cupful of seasoned pumpkin purée; add, with the egg yolks, 1 teaspoonful of vanilla extract. Complete the basic recipe as written.

RAISIN SOUFFLÉ: In 1 cupful of milk, cook 1 cupful of golden raisins, covered, for 15 minutes, or until they are plumped; drain and reserve them. To the cooking milk, add more milk, if necessary, to equal ¾ cupful. To the *roux*, add a grating of nutmeg. Make the *béchamel* with the reserved milk; to it add the reserved raisins. Complete the basic recipe as written.

SOUFFLÉ ROTHSCHILD (TUTTI FRUTTI): In 1 cupful of milk, cook ½ cupful of mixed candied fruit, covered, for 15 minutes; drain and reserve it. To the cooking milk, add more milk, if necessary, to equal ¾ cupful. Make the *béchamel* with the reserved milk; to it, add the reserved fruit and ¼ cupful of dark rum. Complete the basic recipe as written.

**SOUFFLÉ SARAH BERNHARDT ( WITH MACA-ROONS ) :** Soak 12 macaroons in ½ cupful of orange-flavored liqueur. Crush a few additional macaroons and, with the crumbs, coat the buttered dish. Prepare the soufflé batter as described on page 68; season it with 1 teaspoonful of vanilla extract. Transfer one-half of the batter to the prepared dish; over it gently arrange the 12 liqueur-soaked macaroons; add the remaining batter. Complete the basic recipe as written. (If desired, you may use, in place of the 12 macaroons, diced ladyfingers soaked in the liqueur.)

**SPICE SOUFFLÉ :** To the *roux*, add ¾ teaspoonful of cinnamon, ½ teaspoonful of ground cloves, and 1 teaspoonful of nutmeg. Complete the basic recipe as written.

**STRAWBERRY SOUFFLÉ** (a different soufflé from the cold one on page 92): Sugar the buttered soufflé dish. Hull, rinse, drain, and chop medium-coarse 1 pint of strawberries (to equal about 1 cupful); in a mixing bowl toss the berries with a few grains of salt and sugar to taste, and, if desired, 2 tablespoonfuls of orange-flavored liqueur. Make the *roux* with 3 tablespoonfuls each of butter and flour; make the *béchamel* with ¾ cupful of milk. Into the *béchamel*, beat 4 egg yolks; fold in the strawberry mixture. Complete the basic recipe as written, using 4 egg whites.

**VANILLA SOUFFLÉ :** Add, with the egg yolks, 2 teaspoonfuls of vanilla extract. Complete the basic recipe as written.

*Variation:*

In the prepared dish, arrange a one-half-inch layer of soufflé batter; over it, arrange a layer of diced ladyfingers sprinkled with orange-flavored liqueur; add the remaining soufflé batter. Complete the basic recipe as written.

## Apple Soufflé

6 SERVINGS
PREPARATION: 30 MINUTES
COOKING: 30 MINUTES IN A 375° OVEN

*All the ingredients may be readied ahead and combined according to the directions at the time of cooking.*

Thoroughly butter and sugar a 2-quart soufflé dish.

>    4 tablespoons butter
>    4 tablespoons flour

In a large saucepan, heat the butter and in it, over gentle heat, cook the flour for a few minutes.

>    ½ teaspoon cinnamon
>    ½ teaspoon nutmeg
>    ½ cup milk

Into the *roux*, stir the spices. Gradually add the milk, stirring constantly until the mixture is thickened and smooth (it will be very thick).

>    ½ cup sugar
>    Strained juice of 1 small lemon

Away from the heat, add the sugar and lemon juice, beating the mixture until the sugar is dissolved.

>    4 egg yolks
>    3 large tart apples, peeled and grated medium-fine

Beat in the egg yolks. Stir in the grated apple.

>    5 egg whites, beaten until stiff but not dry

Beat in one-fifth of the egg white; fold in the remainder. Using a rubber spatula, transfer the batter to the prepared dish. Bake the soufflé at 375° for 30 minutes, or until it is well-puffed and golden.

## Chocolate Soufflé

4 SERVINGS
PREPARATION: 25 MINUTES
COOKING: 50 MINUTES IN A 300° OVEN

A *very rich dessert.*

*All the ingredients may be readied ahead and combined according to the directions at the time of cooking.*

Thoroughly butter and sugar a 2-quart soufflé dish.

**⅓ cup light cream**
**1 three-ounce package cream cheese, at room temperature**
**½ cup semisweet chocolate bits**

In a saucepan, combine the cream and cream cheese; over gentle heat, cook the mixture, stirring constantly, until the cheese is melted. Add the chocolate bits, stirring the mixture until it is smooth. (If desired, this step may be done in the top of a double boiler over simmering water.) Remove the pan from the heat.

**3 egg yolks**
**A pinch of salt**

Into the mixture, beat the egg yolks and salt.

**4 egg whites**
**4 tablespoons sugar**

Beat the egg whites until they are frothy; then continue to beat them, adding the sugar 1 tablespoonful at a time. When they are stiff but not dry, fold them into the chocolate mixture. Using a rubber spatula, transfer the batter to the prepared dish. Bake the soufflé at 300° for 50 minutes, or until it is well-puffed and golden.

## Jam or Marmalade Soufflé

6 SERVINGS
PREPARATION: 30 MINUTES
COOKING: 40 MINUTES IN A 375° OVEN

*This recipe is a convenient one, enabling you to offer a dessert soufflé with a minimum of work and made from ingredients you may well have on hand.*

*All the ingredients may be readied ahead and combined according to the directions at the time of cooking.*

Thoroughly butter and sugar a 2-quart soufflé dish.

> 3 tablespoons butter
> 3 tablespoons flour
> ¾ cup milk

In a saucepan, heat the butter and in it, over gentle heat, cook the flour for a few minutes. Gradually add the milk, stirring constantly until the mixture is thickened and smooth.

> 1 twelve-ounce jar marmalade or preserves:

| | |
|---|---|
| APPLE BUTTER | PEACH PRESERVE |
| APRICOT PRESERVE | PINEAPPLE PRESERVE |
| BLACKBERRY PRESERVE | PLUM PRESERVE |
| BLUEBERRY PRESERVE | PRUNE BUTTER |
| CHERRY PRESERVE | RASPBERRY PRESERVE |
| GRAPE PRESERVE | ( BLACK OR RED ) |
| LIME MARMALADE ( SWEET ) | STRAWBERRY PRESERVE |
| ORANGE MARMALADE | |
| ( SWEET ) | |

> ½ to ¾ teaspoon grated lemon or orange rind ( optional )
> ¼ teaspoon almond extract *or* ½ teaspoon lemon or orange
>     extract ( optional )
> Pinch of salt

Into the *béchamel*, stir the preserve of your choice; season the mixture to taste.

> 4 egg yolks

Beat in the egg yolks.

**4 egg whites, beaten until stiff but not dry**

Beat in one-fifth of the egg white; fold in the remainder. Using a rubber spatula, transfer the mixture to the prepared dish. Bake the soufflé at 375° for 30 minutes, or until it is well-puffed and golden.

## Lemon Soufflé

6 SERVINGS
PREPARATION: 30 MINUTES
COOKING: 30 MINUTES IN A 350° OVEN

*Made with sour cream, this soufflé is different from that on page 71.*

*All the ingredients may be readied ahead and combined according to the directions at the time of cooking.*

Thoroughly butter and sugar a 2-quart soufflé dish.

**2 cups sour cream**
**3 tablespoons flour**

In a saucepan, blend the sour cream and flour. Over gentle heat, cook the mixture, stirring constantly, until it is somewhat thickened.

**½ cup sugar**
**Grated rind and strained juice of 1 large lemon**
**A pinch of salt**

Add the sugar, lemon rind and juice, and the salt, stirring until the sugar is dissolved. Remove the mixture from the heat.

**4 egg yolks**

Allow the mixture to cool slightly and then beat in the egg yolks.

**4 egg whites, beaten until stiff but not dry**

Fold in the egg white. Using a rubber spatula, transfer the batter to the prepared dish. Bake the dessert at 350° for 30 minutes, or until it is well-puffed and golden.

## Ricotta Soufflé

6 SERVINGS

PREPARATION: 25 MINUTES (THE PREPARATION TIME DOES NOT INCLUDE
    MACERATING THE FRUIT)

COOKING: 45 MINUTES IN A 350° OVEN

*All the ingredients may be readied ahead and combined according to
the directions at the time of cooking.*

Thoroughly butter and sugar a 2-quart soufflé dish.

**¼ cup mixed candied fruits, chopped fine**
**¼ cup golden raisins**
**⅓ cup dark rum**

In a mixing bowl, combine the candied fruit, raisins, and rum; allow
the fruits to macerate for 30 minutes.

**1 pound ricotta cheese**
**2 tablespoons flour**
**¼ cup sugar**
**A pinch of salt**

In a second mixing bowl, combine the cheese, flour, and seasonings;
beat the mixture until it is smooth.

**3 egg yolks**
**Reserved fruit and rum**

Beat in the yolks and then stir in the fruit and rum.

**5 egg whites, beaten until stiff but not dry**

Beat in one-fifth of the egg white; fold in the remainder. Using a rubber spatula, transfer the batter to the prepared dish. Bake the soufflé
at 350° for 45 minutes, or until it is well-puffed and golden.

## Salzburger Nockerln

4 SERVINGS
PREPARATION: 30 MINUTES
COOKING: 10 TO 12 MINUTES IN A 350° OVEN

*All the ingredients may be readied ahead and combined according to the directions at the time of cooking.*

Butter an oblong baking dish 8 × 10 × 2 inches.

**2 egg yolks**
**½ teaspoon grated lemon rind**
**1 teaspoon vanilla extract**
**1 tablespoon flour**

In a mixing bowl, combine the egg yolks, lemon rind, and vanilla extract. With a rotary beater, beat the mixture well, gradually adding the flour as you beat.

**4 egg whites**
**A pinch of salt**
**2 tablespoons sugar**

In a mixing bowl, combine the egg whites and salt. Beat the egg whites until frothy. Continue to beat them, adding the sugar gradually, until they are stiff and satiny.

Beat in one-fifth of the egg white; fold in the remainder.

**Confectioner's sugar**

In the prepared baking dish, make four mounds of the batter; sprinkle them with confectioner's sugar. Bake the Salzburger Nockerln at 350° for 10 to 12 minutes, or until it is golden.

## Sweet Potato Soufflé

6 SERVINGS
PREPARATION: 30 MINUTES (THE PREPARATION TIME DOES NOT INCLUDE
COOKING THE SWEET POTATOES)
COOKING: 30 MINUTES IN A 375° OVEN

*All the ingredients may be readied ahead and combined according to the directions at the time of cooking.*

Thoroughly butter and sugar a 2-quart soufflé dish.

> 6 medium sweet potatoes, scrubbed, boiled for 20 minutes, or
> until very tender, drained, and peeled
> 2 tablespoons sugar

In a mixing bowl, combine the sweet potatoes and sugar and mash
them until they are smooth; sieve them, if desired.

> 3 tablespoons butter
> Grated rind of 1 medium-size lemon

Stir in the butter and lemon rind.

> ⅔ cup milk
> 3 egg yolks
> Salt

Beat in the milk and egg yolks; adjust the seasoning to taste.

> 3 or 4 egg whites, beaten until stiff but not dry

Beat in one-fifth of the egg white; fold in the remainder. Using a
rubber spatula, transfer the batter to the prepared dish. Bake the
soufflé at 375° for 30 minutes, or until it is well-puffed and golden.

> *Crème anglaise*, page 192

*Crème anglaise* is a pleasant complement to this soufflé; if desired,
offer it separately.


## Basic Recipe for Hot Dessert Soufflés (Fruit Base)

4 SERVINGS

PREPARATION: 30 MINUTES (THE PREPARATION TIME WILL VARY DEPEND-
ING UPON HOW MUCH READYING THE MAIN INGREDIENT REQUIRES)
COOKING: 30 MINUTES IN A 350° OVEN

*All the ingredients may be readied ahead and combined according to
the directions at the time of cooking.*

Thoroughly butter and sugar a 1½-quart soufflé dish.

1 cup puréed fruit of your choice, sweetened to taste:

| | |
|---|---|
| APPLE | PEACH |
| APRICOT | PEAR |
| AVOCADO | PLUM |
| BERRY (BLACK—, BLUE—, RASP—, | |
| AND STRAWBERRY) | |

1½ tablespoons lemon juice
A pinch of salt
4 egg yolks
¼ teaspoon almond extract (optional)
1 tablespoon grated orange rind (optional)

Into the fruit purée, beat the lemon juice, salt, egg yolks, and seasonings, if desired.

4 or 5 egg whites, beaten until stiff but not dry

Beat in one-fifth of the egg white; fold in the remainder. Using a rubber spatula, transfer the batter to the prepared dish and place in a pan of hot water. Bake the soufflé at 350° for 30 minutes, or until it is well-puffed and golden.

# Cold Dessert Soufflés and Mousses

Cold dessert soufflés and mousses are made light and airy by the addition of beaten egg white or whipped cream or both; a gelatin base assures their holding their shape. In this book, most cold dessert mousses omit whipped cream; if you fancy adding it to the recipe, do so—the addition will make the dish richer but will change appreciably neither its taste nor consistency.

When making a cold soufflé, you can create quite a dramatic effect by using a 1½-quart soufflé dish and increasing its capacity with a collar of lightly oiled foil. To make the collar, measure the length of foil needed to go around the dish, allowing at least a one-inch overlap. Fold the foil in half lengthwise, oil the upside surface lightly but evenly with tasteless vegetable oil, then wrap the foil, oiled side in, around the dish and secure it with masking or cellophane tape. Fill the dish with the prepared cold soufflé mixture and chill the dessert as directed. When serving it, remove the collar and the soufflé will stand, beautiful and appetizing, above the rim of the dish. If, on the other hand, you prefer not to use a collar, stay with a 2-quart soufflé or other dish, which will be nearly filled; this method also makes a pleasant presentation. From either dish, the dessert will taste the same; but in both instances, chill the dish before filling it.

The time required to chill the custard-gelatin mixture "until it just begins to set," or until it is the consistency of heavy syrup, varies for two reasons: the temperature of the liquid itself (was dissolved gelatin stirred into a chilled custard—unlikely in the making of a cold dessert soufflé—or was softened gelatin stirred into the hot custard—the cus-

82

tomary procedure?) and the temperature of the added ingredient or ingredients (if chilled, the near-jelling time will be considerably reduced). After the custard-gelatin mixture has reached room temperature and the other ingredient(s) are added, allow about one hour for the mixture to "just begin to set" or to attain the consisency of heavy syrup.

For the cook who wishes to offer a sauce complementary to dessert soufflés and mousses, there are in Chapter IV a number offered; these sauces are a pleasant addition, but no sauce is a *must*. It is only an embellishment. If the soufflé or mousse is of especially delicate flavor, it is best to omit a sauce.

For instructions on unmolding cold dessert mousses, see page 47.

## Basic Recipe for Cold Dessert Soufflés

6 SERVINGS

PREPARATION: 30 MINUTES (THE PREPARATION TIME WILL VARY DEPENDING UPON HOW MUCH READYING THE MAIN INGREDIENT REQUIRES)

CHILLING TIME: 6 HOURS

Chill a serving or 2-quart soufflé dish, or furnish a collar for a 1½-quart soufflé dish.

> 1¾ cups milk
> 3 egg yolks

In the top of a double boiler, over direct heat, scald the milk. In a mixing bowl, beat the egg yolks. Over the yolks, pour the milk in a steady stream, beating the mixture constantly. Return the mixture to the top of the double boiler; place the utensil over simmering water.

> ½ cup sugar
> A pinch of salt

Add the sugar and salt. Cook the mixture, stirring constantly, until it coats the spoon. Remove the custard from the heat.

> 1 envelope unflavored gelatin, softened for 5 minutes in
>    ¼ cup cold water

Add the gelatin, stirring until it is dissolved.

**Prepared major ingredient**
**Seasonings**

Stir in the major ingredient and seasonings, as called for. Transfer the mixture to a mixing bowl, allow it to cool, and then chill it until it just begins to set.

**1 cup heavy cream, whipped**
**3 egg whites, beaten until stiff but not dry**

If necessary, beat the chilled mixture briefly to assure its smoothness. Fold in the whipped cream. Beat in one-fifth of the egg white; fold in the remainder. Using a rubber spatula, transfer the mixture to the prepared dish. Chill the soufflé for at least 6 hours, or until it is thoroughly set.

*Crème anglaise,* page 192 (optional)

If you wish to offer a sauce with the dessert, *crème anglaise* goes well with virtually every cold soufflé; other sauces are suggested on pages 191–193.

APPLE SOUFFLÉ: Reduce the milk to 1 cupful; to the custard, after dissolving the gelatin, add 3 tart apples, peeled, grated, and tossed with the strained juice of 1 medium-size lemon, and 1 teaspoonful of vanilla extract. Complete the basic recipe as written.

AVOCADO SOUFFLÉ: Reduce the milk to 1 cupful; to the custard, after dissolving the gelatin, add 2 ripe avocados, peeled, seeded, chopped coarse, and puréed in the container of a food processor or blender, and the strained juice and grated rind of 1 small lemon. Complete the basic recipe as written.

BANANA SOUFFLÉ: To the custard, after dissolving the gelatin, add 2 large, *very* ripe bananas, peeled and puréed, and ½ teaspoonful of vanilla extract. Complete the basic recipe as written.

BLUEBERRY SOUFFLÉ: Reduce the milk to 1 cupful; increase the gelatin to 1½ envelopes; to the custard after dissolving the gelatin, add 2 cupfuls blueberries, stewed, covered, for 20 minutes in ⅓ cupful of water and sieved, and the strained juice of ½ medium-size lemon. Complete the basic recipe as written.

BRANDY ALEXANDER SOUFFLÉ: Reduce the milk to 1 cupful; reduce the sugar to ¼ cupful. To the custard, after dissolving the gelatin, add ½ cupful of Cognac and ¼ cupful of crème de cacao. Complete the basic recipe as written.

BURNT SUGAR SOUFFLÉ: In a heavy skillet, melt and then cook ⅔ cupful sugar until the syrup is golden brown; add ⅔ cupful of water. Continue to cook the syrup, stirring, until it is smooth and reduced to 1 cupful; allow it to cool; combine the syrup with ¾ cupful of milk and the egg yolks; omit the sugar called for in the basic recipe. To the custard, after dissolving the gelatin, add ½ teaspoonful of vanilla extract. Complete the basic recipe as written.

CARROT SOUFFLÉ: Reduce the milk to 1 cupful; to the custard, after dissolving the gelatin, add 1 cupful of carrot purée, seasoned to taste with cinnamon and nutmeg, and ½ teaspoonful of vanilla extract. Complete the basic recipe as written.

CHEESE SOUFFLÉ: Increase the sugar to ⅔ cupful; increase the gelatin to 1½ envelopes softened in ½ cupful of water. To the custard, add, with the softened gelatin, ½ cupful of grated Münster cheese and 1 three-ounce package cream cheese, diced (both cheeses should be at room temperature), and the strained juice and grated rind of 1 medium-size lemon. Stir the mixture until the cheeses are melted. Complete the basic recipe as written.

CHERRY SOUFFLÉ: Drain 1 one-pound can of pitted dark sweet cherries, reserving the liquid; chop the cherries coarse; to the liquid, add milk to equal 1½ cups. Reduce the sugar to ¼ cupful; to the custard, after dissolving the gelatin, add the reserved cherries and a drop or two of almond extract. Complete the basic recipe as written.

CHOCOLATE SOUFFLÉ: Reduce the milk to 1¼ cupfuls; in it, over simmering water, melt 1 six-ounce package semisweet chocolate bits. Reduce the sugar to ¼ cupful; to the custard, add, with the softened gelatin, 1 teaspoonful of vanilla extract. Complete the basic recipe as written.

COCONUT SOUFFLÉ: Omit the sugar entirely and make the custard with 1 fifteen-ounce can "cream of coconut" (cream of coconut is available at specialty food shops and at many supermarkets). To the custard, add, with the softened gelatin, the strained juice and grated rind of 1 medium-size lemon. Complete the basic recipe as written. Just before serving, garnish the soufflé with ¼ cupful of toasted shredded coconut.

COFFEE SOUFFLÉ: To the custard, after dissolving the gelatin, add 4 tablespoonfuls of instant coffee powder and 1 teaspoonful of vanilla extract. Complete the basic recipe as written.

CONCORD GRAPE SOUFFLÉ: Stem and rinse 1½ pounds of Concord grapes. In a saucepan, combine them with ¼ cupful of water and simmer them, covered, for 15 minutes, or until the skins are very tender; sieve them. Measure the purée and to it, if necessary, add scalded milk to equal 1¾ cupfuls. To the custard after dissolving the gelatin, add a drop or two of almond extract. Complete the basic recipe as written.

EGGNOG SOUFFLÉ: Reduce the milk to 1½ cupfuls. To the custard, add, with the softened gelatin, a generous grating of nutmeg and ¼ cupful of bourbon whisky or dark rum. Complete the basic recipe as written; garnish the chilled soufflé with an additional grating of nutmeg.

FIG SOUFFLÉ: Drain thoroughly 2 one-pound cans of Kadota figs; reserve ¾ cup of the liquid; in the container of a food processor or blender, purée the figs. To the liquid add ½ cupful of milk; omit the sugar. To the custard, after dissolving the gelatin, add the fig purée and ½ teaspoonful of vanilla extract. Complete the basic recipe as written.

GINGER SOUFFLÉ I: Reduce the milk to 1½ cupfuls. To the custard, add, with the softened gelatin, ¼ cupful of light rum and ¾ cupful of fine-chopped crystallized ginger. Complete the basic recipe as written.

GINGER SOUFFLÉ II: Reduce the sugar to ¼ cupful. To the custard, after dissolving the gelatin, add 1 cupful of ginger marmalade and ½ teaspoonful of vanilla extract. Complete the basic recipe as written.

GRAND MARNIER SOUFFLÉ: Increase the gelatin to 1½ envelopes, softened in ½ cupful of water. To the custard, add, with the gelatin, ⅓ cupful of Grand Mariner (or other orange-flavored liqueur) and the grated rind of 1 small orange. Complete the basic recipe as written.

GRAPEFRUIT SOUFFLÉ: In the container of a food processor or blender, whirl until smooth the flesh of 2 large seeded grapefruit (pink grapefruit provides a pleasing color); use this purée in place of the milk. Increase the sugar to ¾ cupful. To the custard, after dissolving the gelatin, add 1 tablespoonful of grated orange rind and ½ teaspoonful of orange extract. Complete the basic recipe as written.

GUAVA SOUFFLÉ: Drain 1 fifteen-ounce can of guava shells, reserving the liquid; in the container of a food processor or blender, purée the shells. To the liquid, add milk to equal 1½ cups; reduce the sugar to ¼ cupful. To the custard, after dissolving the gelatin, add guava purée and a drop or two of almond extract. Complete the basic recipe as written.

JAM OR MARMALADE SOUFFLÉ (This recipe enables you to offer a cold dessert soufflé made from ingredients you may well have on hand.): Reduce the milk to 1 cupful; omit the sugar. To the custard, after dissolving the gelatin, add 1 twelve-ounce jar of marmalade or preserves:

**APPLE BUTTER**
**APRICOT PRESERVE**
**BLACKBERRY PRESERVE**
**BLUEBERRY PRESERVE**
**CHERRY PRESERVE**
**GRAPE PRESERVE**
**LIME MARMALADE (SWEET)**
**ORANGE MARMALADE (SWEET)**
**PEACH PRESERVE**
**PINEAPPLE PRESERVE**
**PLUM PRESERVE**
**PRUNE BUTTER**
**RASPBERRY PRESERVE (BLACK OR RED)**
**STRAWBERRY PRESERVE**

Add a drop or two of almond extract. Complete the basic recipe as written.

KUMQUAT SOUFFLÉ: Reduce the milk to 1 cupful; reduce the sugar to ¼ cupful. To the custard, after dissolving the gelatin, add 1½ cupfuls of kumquat purée, page 197, and a drop or two of almond extract. Complete the basic recipe as written.

LEMON SOUFFLÉ: Soften the gelatin in the strained juice of 2 large lemons; grate and reserve the rind. To the custard, add, with the softened gelatin, the reserved lemon rind. Complete the basic recipe as written. (If you want a stronger lemon flavor, add to the custard ¾ to 1 teaspoonful of lemon extract.)

*Variation:*

An unusual dessert may be made by adding to the completed recipe, before chilling it, 1½ cupfuls of melon balls, drained in a colander. Fold them in quickly and gently; chill the soufflé at once.

LIME SOUFFLÉ: Soften the gelatin in the strained juice of 3 limes; grate and reserve the rind of 1 large lime. To the custard, add, with the softened gelatin, the grated lime rind. Complete the basic recipe as written.

MACADAMIA NUT SOUFFLÉ: To the custard, add, with the softened gelatin, 1 cupful of crushed macadamia nuts and 1½ teaspoonfuls of vanilla extract. Complete the basic recipe as written.

MACAROON SOUFFLÉ: To the custard, after dissolving the gelatin, add 12 crushed macaroons soaked in ¼ cupful of orange-flavored liqueur. Complete the basic recipe as written.

MANGO SOUFFLÉ: Drain 1 fifteen-ounce can of sliced mango, reserving the liquid; in the container of a food processor or blender, purée the mango; to the liquid, add milk to equal 1 cup. Reduce the sugar to ¼ cupful. To the custard, after dissolving the gelatin, add the mango purée and ¼ teaspoonful of almond extract. Complete the basic recipe as written.

**MAPLE SOUFFLÉ**: Reduce the milk to 1 cupful; omit the sugar and in its place use ¾ cupful of pure maple syrup. To the custard, add, with the softened gelatin, the strained juice of ½ lemon. Complete the basic recipe as written.

**MELON SOUFFLÉ**: Omit the milk; reduce the sugar to ⅓ cupful. Make the custard with 1¾ cupfuls of purée of very ripe cantaloupe or honeydew melon, adding to the custard with the softened gelatin 1 tablespoonful of strained lemon juice or 3 drops of almond extract. Complete the basic recipe as written.

**MINT-FLAVORED SOUFFLÉ**: Follow the directions for Rosemary-Flavored Soufflé, page 91, using ½ cupful of mint leaves, packed tight, in place of the rosemary; if desired, add a few drops of green food coloring. Complete the basic recipe as written.

**MOCHA SOUFFLÉ**: Melt 2 squares (2 ounces) of unsweetened chocolate in ⅓ cupful of water. Reduce the milk to 1½ cupfuls; increase the sugar to ⅔ cupful; add the milk to the chocolate and proceed with the custard. To the chocolate custard, after dissolving the gelatin, add 1 tablespoonful of instant coffee powder. Complete the basic recipe as written.

**MOLASSES SOUFFLÉ**: Reduce the milk to 1¼ cupfuls; reduce the sugar to ¼ cupful. To the custard, after dissolving the gelatin, add ½ cupful of dark molasses and 2 tablespoonfuls of dark rum. Complete the basic recipe as written.

**NUTMEG SOUFFLÉ**: To the custard, add, with the softened gelatin, 1½ teaspoonfuls of fresh-grated nutmeg and 1 teaspoonful of vanilla extract. Complete the basic recipe as written.

**ORANGE SOUFFLÉ**: To the custard, add, with the softened gelatin, the strained juice and grated rind of 1 large orange and 1 six-ounce can frozen orange juice concentrate, fully thawed to room temperature. Complete the basic recipe as written.

**PAPAYA SOUFFLÉ**: Drain 1 fifteen-ounce can of sliced papaya, reserving the liquid. In the container of a food processor or blender, purée the papaya; to the liquid, add milk to equal 1 cup;

reduce the sugar to ¼ cupful. To the custard, after dissolving the gelatin, add the papaya purée and a drop or two of almond extract. Complete the basic recipe as written.

PEACH SOUFFLÉ: Peel, seed, and purée 4 or 5 ripe peaches (to equal 2 cupfuls); use this purée in place of the milk to make the custard. To the custard, after dissolving the gelatin, add ¼ teaspoonful of almond extract. Complete the basic recipe as written.

PEANUT BRITTLE SOUFFLÉ: To the custard, after dissolving the gelatin, add 1 teaspoonful of vanilla extract. After the addition of the egg white, fold in quickly but gently 1½ cupfuls of crushed peanut brittle. Chill the soufflé immediately.

PEAR SOUFFLÉ: Drain 1 one-pound can of Bartlett pears, reserving the liquid; in the container of a food processor or blender, purée the pears. To the liquid, add milk to equal 1 cup; reduce the sugar to ¼ cupful. To the custard, after dissolving the gelatin, add the pear purée and a drop or two of almond extract. Complete the basic recipe as written.

PEPPERMINT STICK SOUFFLÉ: Reduce the sugar to ¼ cupful. To the custard, after dissolving the gelatin, add ½ teaspoonful of peppermint extract and, if desired, a few drops of green or red food coloring; after the addition of the egg white, fold in quickly but gently ¾ cup of crushed peppermint stick candy. Chill the soufflé immediately.

PERSIMMON SOUFFLÉ: Increase the sugar to ¾ cupful; reduce the milk to 1 cupful. To the custard, after dissolving the gelatin, add the purée of 3 large, very ripe persimmons and a drop or two of almond extract. Complete the basic recipe as written.

PINEAPPLE SOUFFLÉ: In a saucepan, cook 1 cupful of fresh pineapple purée for 5 minutes; reserve it. Increase the gelatin to 1½ envelopes; to the custard, add, with the softened gelatin, the reserved pineapple and ½ teaspoonful of vanilla extract. Complete the basic recipe as written.

PRUNE SOUFFLÉ: Seed and purée with their liquid the prunes from 1 one-pound jar; make the custard using the purée as the total liquid ingredient (omit both the milk and sugar—the purée will be sufficiently sweet). To the custard, after dissolving the gelatin, add the strained juice of 1 small lemon and a drop or two of almond extract. Complete the basic recipe as written.

**PUMPKIN SOUFFLÉ:** Reduce the milk to ¾ cupful; reduce the sugar to ⅓ cupful; increase the gelatin to 2 envelopes, softened in ⅓ cupful of cold water. To the custard, after dissolving the gelatin, add 1 seventeen-ounce can of pumpkin purée seasoned with ½ teaspoonful each of cinnamon, ground cloves, and mace. Complete the basic recipe as written.

**QUINCE SOUFFLÉ:** Drain 1 fifteen-ounce can of quinces, reserving the liquid. In the container of a food processor or blender, purée the quinces; to the liquid, add milk to equal 1 cup; reduce the sugar to ⅓ cupful. To the custard, after dissolving the gelatin, add the quince purée and ¼ teaspoonful of almond extract. Complete the basic recipe as written.

**RHUBARB SOUFFLÉ:** Cook 1½ pounds rhubarb, rinsed and cut into two-inch pieces, in ½ cupful of orange juice for ten minutes, or until very tender; allow it to cool; in the container of a food processor or blender, purée it. Omit the milk, using the purée in its place; increase the sugar to ¾ cupful. To the custard, after dissolving the gelatin, add ½ teaspoonful of cinnamon. Complete the basic recipe as written.

**ROSEMARY-FLAVORED SOUFFLÉ** (best made with fresh leaves, albeit dried ones substitute adequately): In the milk, simmer ¼ to ⅓ cupful bruised rosemary leaves, packed tight, for 10 minutes; strain the milk, discarding the leaves. Complete the basic recipe as written.

**RUM SOUFFLÉ:** Increase the sugar to ⅓ cupful and mix with it 1 tablespoonful of cornstarch; use 1 cupful of light cream and ¾ cupful of milk. To the custard, after dissolving the gelatin, add ⅓ cupful of dark rum and ½ teaspoonful of vanilla extract. Complete the basic recipe as written.

**SPICE SOUFFLÉ:** Mix the sugar with ¾ teaspoonful of cinnamon, ½ teaspoonful of ground cloves, ½ teaspoonful of ground ginger, and 1 teaspoonful of nutmeg; to the custard, add, with the softened gelatin, 1 teaspoonful of vanilla extract. Complete the basic recipe as written.

**STRAWBERRY SOUFFLÉ:** Hull, rinse, and purée 1 quart of ripe strawberries; to the purée, add milk to equal 2 cups and use this mixture to make the custard. To the custard, after dissolving the gelatin, add 2 drops of almond extract. Complete the basic recipe as written.

**TARRAGON-FLAVORED SOUFFLÉ:** Follow the directions for Rosemary-Flavored Soufflés, page 91, using fresh or dried tarragon leaves in place of rosemary.

**TUTTI FRUTTI SOUFFLÉ:** In the milk, simmer 1 cupful of mixed candied fruits, covered, for 15 minutes; use this mixture to make the custard. To the custard, after dissolving the gelatin, add ¼ cupful dark rum *or* 1 teaspoonful of vanilla extract. Complete the basic recipe as written.

**VANILLA SOUFFLÉ:** To the custard, after dissolving the gelatin, add 2 teaspoonfuls of vanilla extract. Complete the basic recipe as written.

## Soufflé aux Marrons (Chestnut Soufflé)

8 SERVINGS
PREPARATION: 40 MINUTES
CHILLING TIME: 6 HOURS

Chill a serving or 2-quart soufflé dish, or furnish a collar for a 1½-quart soufflé dish.

> 1 seventeen-and-one-half-ounce can sweetened chestnut
>    purée (available at specialty food shops)
> 2 cups milk
> 2 envelopes unflavored gelatin

In a saucepan, combine the chestnut purée and milk; using a rotary beater, blend them until the mixture is smooth. Over the surface, sprinkle the gelatin and allow it to soften for 5 minutes. Over medium heat, bring the purée to the boil, stirring constantly until the gelatin is dissolved.

> 3 egg yolks
> 2 tablespoons dark rum
> ¾ teaspoon vanilla extract
> A pinch of salt

Away from the heat, beat in the egg yolks and seasonings. Over gentle heat, cook the mixture, stirring constantly, until it is slightly thickened. Allow it to cool and then chill it until it just begins to set.

> 1 cup heavy cream, whipped
> 3 egg whites, beaten until stiff but not dry

Fold in the whipped cream. Beat in one-fifth of the egg white; fold in the remainder. Using a rubber spatula, transfer the mixture to the chilled dish. Chill the soufflé for at least 6 hours, or until it is thoroughly set.

## Basic Recipe for Fruit Mousses

8 SERVINGS

PREPARATION: 30 MINUTES (THE PREPARATION TIME WILL VARY DEPENDING
   UPON HOW MUCH READYING THE MAIN INGREDIENT REQUIRES)
CHILLING TIME: 6 HOURS

*This recipe is desiged to be made, in some cases, with convenience foods, thus enabling you to offer the dessert from ingredients you have on hand.*

*You may, if desired, fold 1 cupful of heavy cream, whipped, into the chilled fruit mixture before the addition of the egg white.*

Lightly oil and chill a 6-cup ring or other mold; or chill a serving dish.

> 1 envelope unflavored gelatin, softened for 5 minutes in ¼
>    cup cold water

Over simmering water, dissolve the gelatin and reserve it.

Fruit ingredient of your
   choice (see below) and its
   liquid or liquid ingredient
Sugar
Strained juice of 1 small
   lemon

1 teaspoon vanilla
   extract *or* a drop or
   two of almond
   extract (both
   optional)
A pinch of salt
Reserved gelatin

In a mixing bowl, sweeten the fruit ingredient to taste; add the lemon juice, seasonings, and gelatin. Stir the mixture to blend it well and to dissolve the sugar. Chill it until it just begins to set.

**3 egg whites, beaten until stiff but not dry**

Into the mixture, beat one-fifth of the egg white; fold in the remainder. Using a rubber spatula, transfer the mixture to the prepared mold or dish. Chill the mousse for at least 6 hours, or until it is thoroughly set. Unmold the mousse onto a chilled serving plate or serve it directly from the dish.

Brandy-and-Lemon Sauce or *Crème anglaise*, page 192, is pleasant with cold fruit mousses.

APRICOT: 2 cups purée.

AVOCADO: 2 large ripe avocados, peeled, seeded, and puréed; ¾ cup milk; a few drops green food coloring.

BLACKBERRY: 1 quart berries, rinsed, drained, and sieved, plus milk to equal 2 cups.

BLUEBERRY: 2 cups berries, cooked in ½ cup water until they burst, then puréed and cooled, plus milk, if necessary, to equal 2 cups.

CHERRY: Drain 1 one-pound can dark sweet cherries; chop the fruit coarse. To the liquid, add milk to equal 2 cups.

MELON: Puréed flesh of large ripe cantaloupe or honeydew, plus milk, if necessary, to equal 2 cups.

ORANGE: Juice and grated rind of 1 orange, plus 1 six-ounce can frozen orange juice concentrate, fully thawed to room temperature; add water to equal 2 cups.

PEACH: 2 cups purée prepared from ripe peaches.

PEAR: 2 cups purée prepared from ripe pears, *or* purée 1 one-pound can Bartlett pears with their liquid and add milk to equal 2 cups.

PINEAPPLE: Drain 1 one-pound can crushed pineapple; to the liquid add milk to equal 2 cups.

PLUM: 1 one-pound jar of purple plums, seeded and puréed, with their liquid.

PRUNE: Follow the directions for Plum Soufflé (above).

PUMPKIN: 1½ cups seasoned pumpkin purée plus ½ cup milk.

RASPBERRY: 2 ten-ounce packages frozen raspberries, fully thawed to room temperature and sieved, plus milk, if necessary, to equal 2 cups.

STRAWBERRY: 1 quart berries, hulled, rinsed, drained, and sieved, plus strained fresh orange juice, if necessary, to equal 2 cups.

DRIED FRUIT: 1 eleven-ounce package mixed dried fruits, cooked according to the directions on the package, seeded, and puréed with their liquid (2 cups).

## Apple Mousse

6 SERVINGS
PREPARATION: 30 MINUTES
CHILLING TIME: 6 HOURS

Chill a 6-cup ring mold.

**Juice and grated rind of 1 large lemon**
**4 large tart apples, peeled**

Into a mixing bowl containing the lemon juice and rind, grate the apples. Stir each addition of apple so that it is well mixed with the lemon juice in order to prevent its discoloring.

> ½ cup strained orange juice
> 1 envelope unflavored gelatin

In the orange juice, soften the gelatin for 5 minutes and then dissolve it over simmering water. Stir it into the apple mixture.

> ¾ cup sugar
> ¾ teaspoon cinnamon
> ¾ teaspoon nutmeg
> 1 teaspoon vanilla extract
> A pinch of salt

Into the apple mixture, stir the sugar and seasonings. When the sugar is dissolved, chill the mixture until it just begins to set.

> 1 cup heavy cream, whipped

Fold in the whipped cream. Using a rubber spatula, transfer the mixture to the prepared mold rinsed with cold water. Chill the mousse for 6 hours, or until it is thoroughly set.

> *Crème anglaise*, page 192

Unmold the mousse onto a chilled serving plate and offer the sauce separately.

*Variation:*

APPLE AND BLACKBERRY MOUSSE: Simmer 1½ cupfuls of blackberries, covered, for 10 minutes in ¼ cupful of water; sieve the berries; use 1½ envelopes of unflavored gelatin softened in the orange juice and then dissolved in the hot blackberry purée. Complete the recipe as written.


## *Apricot Mousse*

6 SERVINGS
PREPARATION: 45 MINUTES
CHILLING TIME: 6 HOURS

Chill a 5-cup serving bowl.

> 1½ envelopes unflavored gelatin, softened for 5 minutes in
> ¼ cup cold water

Over simmering water, dissolve the gelatin; reserve it.

   1 eight-ounce package tenderized dried apricots
   3 cups water
   ½ cup sugar
   A pinch of salt

In a saucepan, combine the apricots, water, sugar, and salt; bring the liquid to the boil, reduce the heat, and simmer the apricots, covered, for 30 minutes, or until they are very tender. In the container of a food processor or blender, whirl the apricots and their liquid, 2 cupfuls at a time, until the mixture is smooth. Transfer it to a mixing bowl.

   Strained reserved gelatin juice of 1 small lemon

Stir in the reserved gelatin and the lemon juice. Allow the mixture to cool and then chill it until it just begins to set.

   4 egg whites, beaten until stiff but not dry

Beat in one-fifth of the egg white; fold in the remainder. Using a rubber spatula, transfer the mixture to the prepared dish. Chill the mousse for at least 6 hours, or until it is thoroughly set. Serve it direct from the dish.


## Banana Mousse

6 SERVINGS
PREPARATION: 30 MINUTES
CHILLING TIME: 6 HOURS

Lightly oil and chill a 5-cup ring or other mold.

   1 envelope unflavored gelatin
   ½ cup strained orange juice

Sprinkle the gelatin over the orange juice. Allow it to soften for 5 minutes and then dissolve it over simmering water. Reserve it.

   3 large ripe bananas, peeled         1 teaspoon vanilla
       and chopped coarse                    extract
   Strained juice and grated           A pinch of salt
       rind of 1 lemon                  Reserved gelatin
   ½ cup sugar

In the container of a food processor or blender, combine the bananas, lemon juice and rind, sugar, vanilla, salt, and gelatin. Whirl the mixture until it is smooth. Transfer it to a mixing bowl and chill it until it just begins to set.

>   **1 cup heavy cream, whipped**

Fold in the whipped cream. Using a rubber spatula, transfer the mixture to the prepared mold. Chill the mousse for at least 6 hours, or until it is thoroughly set.

>   **Berry Sauce, page 191**

Unmold the mousse onto a chilled serving plate. Offer the sauce separately.


## Blue-Cheese and Pear Mousse

6 SERVINGS
PREPARATION: 35 MINUTES
CHILLING TIME: 6 HOURS

Lightly oil and chill a 5-cup ring or other mold.

>   **1 envelope unflavored gelatin**
>   **1 one-pound can of pears**

Soften the gelatin for 5 minutes in the liquid from the pears, then dissolve it over simmering water and reserve it. Drain the pears on absorbent paper and then cut them into small dice; reserve them.

>   **6 ounces blue cheese, at room temperature**
>   **3 ounces cream cheese, at room temperature**
>   **A pinch of salt**
>   **Reserved gelatin**
>   **Sugar**

In a mixing bowl, combine the blue and cream cheeses, salt, and gelatin; with a rotary beater, whip the mixture until it is light. Add sugar, if desired, to taste; continue beating the mixture until the sugar is dissolved. Chill the mixture until it just begins to set.

>   **1 cup heavy cream, whipped**
>   **Reserved pears**

Fold in the whipped cream. Arrange the pear dice in an even layer on the bottom of the mold. Using a rubber spatula, transfer the cheese mixture to the mold. Chill the mousse for at least 6 hours, or until it is thoroughly set. Unmold the mousse onto a chilled serving plate.

*Variation:*

If desired, the pear dice may be folded, quickly and gently, into the cheese mixture immediately after the addition of the whipped cream.

## Chestnut Mousse

6 TO 8 SERVINGS
PREPARATION: 30 MINUTES
CHILLING TIME: 6 HOURS

Lightly oil and chill a 6-cup ring or other mold.

> 2 envelopes unflavored gelatin
> ½ cup cold milk

Soften the gelatin in the milk for 5 minutes and then dissolve it over simmering water. Reserve it.

> 1 fifteen-and-one-half-ounce can sweetened chestnut purée (available at specialty food stores)
> 1½ cups milk
>
> 2 tablespoons dark rum
> 1 teaspoon vanilla extract
> A pinch of salt
> Reserved gelatin

In a mixing bowl, combine the chestnut purée, milk, rum, seasonings, and gelatin. With a rotary beater, blend the mixture until it is smooth. Chill it until it just begins to set.

> 5 egg whites, beaten until stiff but not dry

Using a rotary beater, whip the chestnut mixture to eliminate any possible lumps. Beat in one-fifth of the egg white; fold in the remainder. Using a rubber spatula, transfer the mixture to the prepared mold. Chill the mousse for at least 6 hours, or until it is thoroughly set.

*Crème anglaise,* page 192

Unmold the mousse onto a chilled serving plate. Offer the sauce separately.

*Variation:*

If desired, 1 cupful of heavy cream, whipped, may be folded into the chestnut mixture before the addition of the egg white; the result is almost indecently delicious.


## *Chocolate Mousse*

6 SERVINGS
PREPARATION: 30 MINUTES
CHILLING TIME: 6 HOURS

Chill a 5-cup serving dish.

> **2 squares unsweetened chocolate**
> **½ cup confectioners sugar**

In a saucepan, over gentle heat, melt the chocolate; stir in the sugar. Reserve the mixture.

> **1 envelope unflavored gelatin, softened for 5 minutes in ¼**
> **cup cold water**

Over simmering water, dissolve the gelatin and reserve it.

> **1 cup milk**                     **A pinch of salt**
> **¾ cup sugar**                    **Reserved chocolate**
> **1 teaspoon vanilla**             **Reserved gelatin**

In a saucepan, scald the milk; to it add the sugar, seasonings, chocolate, and gelatin, stirring until the sugar is melted. Transfer the mixture to a mixing bowl, allow it to cool, and then chill it until it just begins to set.

> **2 cups heavy cream, whipped**

Fold in the whipped cream. With a rubber spatula, transfer the mixture to the prepared dish. Chill the mousse for at least 6 hours, or until it is thoroughly set. Serve it directly from the dish.

## Chocolate-Orange Mousse

6 SERVINGS
PREPARATION: 40 MINUTES
CHILLING TIME: 6 HOURS

Chill a 6-cup ring mold or serving dish.

**1 envelope unflavored gelatin**
**Strained juice of 1 large orange**

Soften the gelatin in the orange juice for 5 minutes and then dissolve it over simmering water; reserve it.

**2 eggs**
**½ cup sugar**

In a mixing bowl, combine the eggs and sugar. Using a rotary beater, beat the mixture until it is satiny and lemon-colored. Reserve it.

**1 six-ounce package semisweet chocolate bits**
**¼ cup water**

In a saucepan, combine the chocolate bits and water. Over gentle heat, dissolve the chocolate, stirring constantly.

**¼ cup orange-flavored liqueur**
**Grated rind of 1 large orange**
**Reserved gelatin**
**Reserved egg mixture**

Into the contents of the saucepan, stir the liqueur, orange rind, gelatin, and egg mixture. Transfer the mixture to a mixing bowl and chill it until it just begins to set.

**1 cup heavy cream, whipped**

Fold in the whipped cream. Using a rubber spatula, transfer the mixture to the prepared mold or serving dish. Chill the mousse for at least 6 hours, or until it is thoroughly set.

***Crème anglaise*, page 192**

Unmold the mousse onto a chilled serving plate or serve it directly from the dish. Offer the sauce separately.

## Chutney Mousse

6 SERVINGS
PREPARATION: 35 MINUTES
CHILLING TIME: 6 HOURS

Lightly oil and chill a 5-cup ring or other mold.

> 1½ envelopes unflavored gelatin
> 1 cup orange juice

Soften the gelatin in the orange juice for 5 minutes and then dissolve it over simmering water. Reserve it.

> 1 eight-and-one-half-ounce jar mango chutney
> Juice and grated rind of 1 medium-size lemon
> ½ cup sugar
>
> 1 teaspoon vanilla extract
> A pinch of salt
> Reserved gelatin

In the container of a food processor or blender, combine the chutney, lemon juice and rind, sugar, seasonings, and gelatin. Whirl them until the mixture is smooth. Transfer it to a mixing bowl and chill it until it just begins to set.

> 1 cup heavy cream, whipped

Fold in the whipped cream. Using a rubber spatula, transfer the mixture to the prepared mold. Chill the mousse for at least 6 hours, or until it is thoroughly set.

> Crème anglaise, page 192

Unmold the mousse onto a chilled serving plate. Offer the sauce separately.


## Coconut Mousse

6 SERVINGS
PREPARATION: 25 MINUTES
CHILLING TIME: 6 HOURS

Lightly oil and chill a 5-cup ring or other mold.

1½ envelopes unflavored gelatin, softened for 5 minutes in
⅓ cup cold water

Over simmering water, dissolve the gelatin; reserve it.

| | |
|---|---|
| 1 fifteen-ounce can "cream of coconut" (available at specialty food stores and many supermarkets) | 1 teaspoon vanilla extract A pinch of salt A few drops of yellow food coloring |
| 1 cup milk | Reserved gelatin |

In a mixing bowl, combine the cream of coconut, milk, vanilla extract, salt, food coloring, and gelatin. With a rotary beater, blend the mixture well and then chill it until it just begins to set.

1 cup heavy cream, whipped
Toasted shredded coconut (optional)

Fold in the whipped cream. Using a rubber spatula, transfer the mixture to the prepared mold. Chill the mousse for at least 6 hours, or until it is thoroughly set. Unmold it onto a chilled serving plate and garnish it, if desired, with a sprinkling of toasted shredded coconut.

## Cranberry Mousse

6 SERVINGS
PREPARATION: 30 MINUTES
CHILLING TIME: 6 HOURS

Chill a 5-cup ring or other mold.

1½ envelopes unflavored gelatin, softened for 5 minutes in
¼ cup cold water

Over simmering water, dissolve the gelatin and reserve it.

| | |
|---|---|
| 3 cups cranberries, rinsed and drained | Grated rind of 1 orange Juice and grated rind of |
| ¾ cup sugar | 1 medium-size lemon |
| 1½ cups orange juice | A pinch of salt |

In a saucepan, combine the cranberries, sugar, orange juice and rind, lemon juice and rind, and salt. Bring the liquid to the boil, reduce the heat, and cook the cranberries, covered, for about 10 minutes, or until they have burst and are tender.

**Reserved gelatin**

Stir in the reserved gelatin. Transfer the mixture to a mixing bowl and chill it until it just begins to set.

**1 cup heavy cream, whipped**

Fold in the whipped cream. Using a rubber spatula, transfer the mixture to the prepared mold. Chill the mousse for at least 6 hours, or until it is thoroughly set. Unmold onto a chilled serving plate.

A second recipe for Cranberry Mousse appears on page 106.

## Kumquat Mousse

6 SERVINGS

PREPARATION: 20 MINUTES (THE PREPARATION TIME DOES NOT INCLUDE READYING THE KUMQUAT PURÉE, PAGE 197)

CHLLING TIME: 6 HOURS

Lightly oil and chill a 5-cup ring or other mold.

**1 envelope unflavored gelatin**
**1 cup orange juice**

Soften the gelatin in the orange juice for 5 minutes and then dissolve it over simmering water. Reserve it.

| | |
|---|---|
| **1 cup kumquat purée** | **A pinch of salt** |
| **¼ cup sugar ( optional )** | **Reserved gelatin** |
| **1 teaspoon vanilla extract** *or* | |
| **¼ teaspoon almond** | |
| **extract** | |

In a mixing bowl, combine and blend the purée, sugar, seasonings, and gelatin. When the sugar is dissolved, chill the mixture until it just begins to set.

**1 cup heavy cream, whipped**

Fold in the whipped cream. Using a rubber spatula, transfer the mixture to the prepared mold. Chill the mousse for at least 6 hours, or until it is thoroughly set.

**Brandy-and-Lemon Sauce, page 192**

Unmold the mousse onto a chilled serving plate. Offer the sauce separately.

## Mango Mousse

6 TO 8 SERVINGS
PREPARATION TIME: 25 MINUTES
CHILLING TIME: 6 HOURS

Lightly oil and chill a 6-cup ring or other mold.

**1½ envelopes unflavored gelatin, softened for 5 minutes in
⅓ cup cold water**

Over simmering water, dissolve the gelatin and reserve it.

**2 fifteen-ounce cans sliced
mango, with their liquid
(available at Middle
Eastern, Oriental, and
specialty food stores)
Strained juice of 1 medium-
size lemon**

**3 tablespoons sugar
¼ teaspoon almond
extract
A pinch of salt
Reserved gelatin**

In the container of a food processor or blender, combine the mango and mango liquid, lemon juice, sugar, almond extract, salt, and gelatin. Whirl them until the mixture is smooth. Transfer it to a mixing bowl and chill it until it just begins to set.

**1 cup heavy cream, whipped (optional)
3 egg whites, beaten until stiff but not dry**

Fold in the whipped cream. Beat in one-fifth of the egg white; fold in the remainder. Using a rubber spatula, transfer the mixture to the prepared mold. Chill the mousse for at least 6 hours, or until it is thoroughly set.

**Crème anglaise, page 192**

Unmold the mousse onto a chilled serving plate. Offer the sauce separately.

*Variation:*

CRANBERRY MOUSSE: In place of the mango, use 1 one-pound package cranberries, boiled with 1 cupful of water and 1 cupful of sugar until they burst. Dissolve the softened gelatin in the hot berries; omit the 3 tablespoonfuls of sugar and the lemon juice; add the juice and grated rind of 1 orange. Allow the mixture to cool before puréeing and then chill it until it just begins to set. Complete the recipe as written. This recipe is a little sweeter and considerably smoother than the Cranberry Mousse on page 103.

## Maple Mousse

6 SERVINGS
PREPARATION: 15 MINUTES
CHILLING TIME: 6 HOURS

Lightly oil and chill a 5-cup ring or other mold.

> 1 **envelope unflavored gelatin**
> 1 **cup milk**

Soften the gelatin in the milk for 5 minutes and then dissolve it over simmering water. Reserve it.

> 1 **cup maple syrup**
> **A few grains of salt**
> **Reserved gelatin**

In a mixing bowl, combine the maple syrup, salt, and gelatin. Stir the mixture to blend it well and then chill it until it just begins to set.

> 1 **cup heavy cream, whipped**
> 3 **whites, beaten until stiff but not dry**

Fold in the whipped cream. Beat in one-fifth of the egg white; fold in the remainder. Using a rubber spatula, transfer the mixture to the prepared mold. Chill the mousse for at least 6 hours, or until it is thoroughly set. Unmold it onto a chilled serving plate.

*Variations:*

**APPLESAUCE MOUSSE:** Increase the gelatin to 1½ envelopes; in place of the maple syrup, use 2 cupfuls of seasoned applesauce; add the juice and grated rind of 1 small lemon. Complete the recipe as written.

**HONEY MOUSSE:** In place of the maple syrup, use 1 cupful of honey; add to the gelatin when dissolving in the grated rind of 1 small orange. Complete the recipe as written.

## Mincemeat Mousse

6 TO 8 SERVINGS
PREPARATION: 35 MINUTES
CHILLING TIME: 6 HOURS

Lightly oil and chill a 6-cup ring or other mold.

> 1 nine-ounce package dehydrated mincemeat
> 1½ cups water

Into a saucepan, crumble the mincemeat. Add the water; bring the mixture to the boil and cook it, stirring, for 5 minutes.

> 1 envelope unflavored gelatin
> ¼ cup dark rum
> Juice and grated rind of 1 medium-size lemon

Soften the gelatin in the rum for 5 minutes; add it, together with the lemon juice and rind, to the hot mincemeat, stirring until the gelatin is dissolved. Transfer the mixture to a mixing bowl, allow it to cool, and then chill it until it just begins to set.

> 1 cup heavy cream, whipped

Fold in the whipped cream. Using a rubber spatula, transfer the mixture to the prepared mold. Chill the mousse for at least 6 hours, or until it is thoroughly set.

*Crème anglaise,* page 192

Unmold the mousse onto a chilled serving plate. Offer the sauce separately.


## Frozen Strawberry Mousse

6 SERVINGS
PREPARATION: 30 MINUTES
FREEZING TIME: 3 HOURS

Chill a 5-cup serving bowl.

> **2 egg whites**
> **A pinch of salt**
> **⅔ cup sugar**

In a mixing bowl, combine the egg whites and salt; beat the egg white until it is foamy. Adding the sugar a little at a time, continue beating the egg white until it is stiff.

> **1 quart strawberries, hulled, rinsed, and drained**

In the container of a food processor or blender, whirl the berries until they are reduced to a smooth purée; you may also sieve them. Into the egg-white mixture, fold the purée.

> **1 cup heavy cream, whipped**

Have the whipped cream ready so that you may fold it in immediately after you combine the berries and egg white. Using a rubber spatula, transfer the mixture to the prepared serving dish. Place the mousse in the freezing compartment of the refrigerator for at least 3 hours.

*Variations:*

This mousse may be made with blackberries or raspberries, sieved to eliminate the seeds, or with blueberries (see page 94 for their preparation). Complete the recipe as written.

Another recipe for Strawberry Mousse appears on page 95.

# Jellies

# Jellies

---

The word "aspic," commonly applied to main-dish jellies, does not derive from "asp," as is sometimes thought (the coolness of the dish evoking the coldness of the reptile—awful thought!), but rather from the Greek word *aspis*, which meant "buckler" or "shield," the form in which aspics were first made. "Gelatin," the all-important ingredient, derives from the Latin *gelata*, "cold" or "frozen." A pure protein made from collagen, derived from bones, skins, and the white connective tissue of animals, gelatin is not life-sustaining because it lacks two important amino acids; its nutritive value lies in its complementing other proteins and in its action as an acid neutralizer.

Until 1890, gelatin was made, rather laboriously, at home, chiefly from veal knuckles and bones, but in that year Charles Knox developed production of gelatin in granular form. He was not, to be sure, the first to make it commercially; it had been for sale in France from the latter part of the seventeenth century and, after the French Revolution, was required by law to be offered by public eating places as a nutritional supplement in soups and stews. The measure was unpopular, however, because the gelatin, available in colorless sheets resembling isinglass, was bad-tasting. In Europe, gelatin is still produced in sheets dissolvable in hot liquid.

Two types of gelatin are currently on the market in this country. One is an acid gelatin made from the collagen extracted from animal skins and used in commercially packaged ready-flavored gelatin desserts. The second is alkaline gelatin, made from the collagen extracted from the long bones of cattle; this unflavored gelatin is the variety called for in this book. One envelope is equivalent to 28 calories. In its production, the raw materials are given first a series of dilute acid baths and then a soaking in lime water. The collagen is dissolved in hot water, concentrated, filtered to assure its purity and clarity, cooled, and finally dried into glassy sheets which are broken by high-speed mills into tiny granules suitable for easy use in the home.

There are four ways to dissolve unflavored gelatin, three of which require that the gelatin be softened by soaking for five minutes in cold water (usually ¼ cup of water for each envelope of gelatin). Then it may be dissolved over direct heat, or by placing the container in which it has softened in a pan of simmering water, or by adding very hot liquid to it. The fourth way is to mix the prescribed quantity of gelatin with the designated amount of sugar in a dessert recipe and then stir the sugar mixture into a hot liquid ingredient.

One envelope of gelatin will set about 2 cups of liquid; the measure varies depending upon the firmness desired. Clear gelatin with no added foods sets in about two hours; recipes containing added food require about four hours; layered aspic dishes need about twelve hours to set. I suggest a six-hour chilling time in the refrigerator because I have found that within these rules of thumb for jelling, there can be a wide margin for error. One cannot allow too much time for an aspic to set, while one surely wants to avoid insufficient time and the resultant culinary disappointment.

The time required to chill the gelatin mixture "until it just begins to set," or until it is the consistency of heavy syrup, varies for two reasons: the temperature of the liquid itself (was dissolved gelatin stirred into a chilled liquid or was softened gelatin dissolved in a hot liquid?) and the temperature of the added solid ingredient or ingredients (if they are chilled, as is frequently suggested, the near-jelling time will be considerably reduced). Dissolved gelatin stirred into a chilled liquid to which chilled ingredients are added will "just begin to set" or attain the consistency of heavy syrup in about thirty minutes.

To unmold main-dish aspics or dessert gelatins, loosen all edges with the point of a sharp knife. Have a chilled serving platter at hand, rinsed with cold water. Into very warm, not hot water submerge the mold to the level of the aspic. Count deliberately to eight. Remove the mold, wiping away any excess water; place the platter over it and invert both. Shake gently or place the platter on a firm surface and rap the bottom of the mold sharply two or three times. When the aspic settles onto the platter, center it by easing the mold to the desired position; remove the mold, wipe away any drops of liquid, and return the aspic to the refrigerator.

When making aspics and gelatins, chill all prepared solid ingredients (meats, vegetables, fruits) before adding them to the gelatin mixture, which you have also chilled just to the point of setting (it should be the consistency of raw egg white); this method prevents the solid ingredients from "floating." If you want the aspic to set quickly, place it in the freezer for 25 to 30 minutes and then remove it to the refrigerator; do not allow it to freeze, however, for the water content will separate from the gelatin.

Fresh pineapple contains an enzyme which prevents jelling; either use canned pineapple or parboil the fresh fruit for five minutes.

Plain yogurt substituted for milk in dessert gelatins gives a creamy consistency and a pleasantly tart-sweet taste especially complementary to fruits; to use yogurt, dissolve the softened gelatin and blend it with the yogurt—do not heat the yogurt.

When preparing a molded aspic, rinse the mold with cold water or oil it lightly with a tasteless vegetable oil; this step will facilitate unmolding the finished dish. Use a metal mold for ease in unmolding the aspic; aluminum, which reacts badly to eggs, will neither discolor nor give an unpleasant taste to aspics.

To line a mold with aspic, chill the utensil thoroughly. Prepare the aspic by using one envelope of unflavored gelatin and 1½ cups liquid, flavored to your taste (beef, chicken, Madeira or port wine, etc.); chill the mixture until it is the consistency of a heavy syrup, pour it into the prepared mold, and rotate the mold so that the gelatin covers all surfaces. Place the mold in the freezer until the gelatin just begins to set on the bottom and sides, or, if you prefer, turn the mold in cracked ice; pour off any excess aspic and refrigerate the mold until it is thoroughly set, meanwhile continuing with the recipe at hand. Because the purpose of this book is to offer carefree, easy, and time-saving recipes, aspic-lined molds are not dealt with in specific recipes. They are decorative and elegant, however, and every so often it is fun to offer an aspic as visually elaborate as it is gustatorially splendid.

Aspic-lined molds may be decorated with any of the suggestions offered on page 121. When the lined mold is completely set, virtually any of the aspic recipes may be added to complete the mold, the selection being left to the ingenuity, creativeness, preferences, or just plain daring of the cook.

# Main-Dish Jellies

## Basic Recipe for Main-Dish Aspic

6 TO 8 SERVINGS

PREPARATION: 20 MINUTES (THE PREPARATION TIME DOES NOT INCLUDE
    READYING THE SOLID INGREDIENT)
CHILLING TIME: 6 HOURS

Lightly oil and chill a 5-cup ring or other mold.

| | |
|---|---|
| 2 envelopes unflavored gelatin, softened for 5 minutes in ½ cup cold water | 1 to 1½ cups chilled solid ingredient or ingredients |
| 3½ cups clarified beef, chicken, veal, *or* vegetable stock, *or* fruit juice, pages 115–119, chilled | Seasonings |

Over simmering water, dissolve the gelatin; add it to the stock or juice, stirring to blend the mixture. Chill the aspic until it just begins to set. Add the chilled solid ingredient or ingredients of your choice and such seasonings as may be called for. Transfer the mixture to the prepared mold. Chill the aspic for at least 6 hours, or until it is thoroughly set.

114

Salad greens (optional) *or* composed salad of your choice,
    pages 193–197 (optional)

Unmold the aspic onto a chilled serving plate. Garnish it, if desired, with salad greens or with a composed salad.

## Beef (Brown) Stock

YIELD: ABOUT 1½ QUARTS
PREPARATION: 25 MINUTES
COOKING: 3 HOURS

| | |
|---|---|
| 1½ pounds cracked marrow bone | 1 small turnip, chopped coarse |
| 3 pounds lean beef (shin or other soup meat), chopped coarse | 1 bay leaf |
| | 3 cloves |
| | ½ teaspoon marjoram |
| 1 medium-size carrot, chopped | 4 peppercorns |
| 1 large rib celery with its leaves, chopped | ½ teaspoon thyme |
| | 1 teaspoon sugar |
| 1 clove garlic, split | 1½ teaspoons salt |
| 1 medium-size onion, quartered | 8 cups water |

In a soup kettle, combine all of the ingredients. Bring the liquid to the boil, skimming it as necessary; reduce the heat and simmer the mixture, covered, for 3 hours. Strain it. Allow it to cool and then refrigerate overnight. Clarify it, page 117.

Canned beef broth substitutes nicely for homemade stock; I do not pretend that it is the same, but it *is* time-saving and more economical. Canned consommé madrilene, especially if laced with a little dry sherry, makes a very good stand-in for the homemade product; it has, however, a flavor distinctively its own. Bouillon cubes or powder make an acceptably flavored, if thin, broth upon which these aspic recipes may be based.

## Chicken Stock

YIELD: ABOUT 1½ QUARTS
PREPARATION: 25 MINUTES
COOKING: 2 HOURS

| | |
|---|---|
| 1 four-pound fowl, disjointed | 1 bay leaf |
| 1 medium-size carrot, chopped | 4 peppercorns |
| 2 ribs celery, chopped, with their leaves | 1 teaspoon sugar |
| 1 medium-size onion, quartered | 1 teaspoon salt |
| | 8 cups water |

In a soup kettle, combine all of the ingredients. Bring the liquid to the boil, reduce the heat, and simmer the mixture, covered, for 2 hours. Strain it, reserving the meat for use in another recipe. Allow the stock to cool and then refrigerate it overnight. Clarify it, page 117.

Three ten-and-one-half-ounce cans of defatted chicken broth substitute nicely for homemade stock; as is the case with Beef Stock, page 117, I do not pretend that it is the same, but it is time-saving and, unless you plan to use the chicken meat from the recipe above, very economical. Bouillon cubes or powder make an acceptably flavored, if thin, broth upon which these aspic recipes may be based.

To defat canned chicken broth, place the cans in the refrigerator overnight so that the fat will congeal; upon opening the broth, you may either strain it or remove the congealed fat with a spoon.

## Veal (White) Stock

YIELD: ABOUT 1½ QUARTS
PREPARATION: 25 MINUTES
COOKING: 4½ HOURS

1 three-pound veal knuckle,
   cut into small pieces
1 medium rib celery,
   chopped, with its leaves
1 medium carrot, chopped
1 medium onion, quartered
1 small bay leaf
2 cloves

A blade of mace
   (optional) or ¼
   teaspoon ground mace
   or nutmeg
4 peppercorns
½ teaspoon thyme
1 teaspoon sugar
1 tablespoon salt
8 cups water

In a soup kettle, combine all of the ingredients. Bring the liquid to the boil, skimming it as necessary; reduce the heat and simmer the mixture, covered, for 4½ hours. Strain it. Allow it to cool and then refrigerate it overnight. Clarify it (below).

TO CLARIFY STOCK: Remove any solidified fat from chilled meat stock; discard it. Pour the stock into a saucepan. To it, add 1 egg white and 2 tablespoonfuls of cold water, beaten together with a fork, and the crushed eggshell. Bring the stock to the boil for 2 minutes, stirring constantly; reduce the heat to the lowest level and allow the stock to stand for 20 minutes. Strain the stock through a fine strainer lined with two layers of cheesecloth.

VEGETABLE STOCK is a home product—easy, economical, nutritious, and kind to the calorie counter. Rinse or scrub all vegetables, dry them on absorbent paper (excess moisture hastens spoiling, even under refrigeration), peel or scrape the vegetable, collect and refrigerate the peelings. When you have collected a good quantity of peelings —let us say, 4 handfuls—put them in a large saucepan with a large onion, quartered, a clove of garlic, split, a bay leaf or two, some other herb of your choice, and a little sugar, salt, and pepper; add water to cover by 1 inch, bring the liquid to the boil, reduce the heat, and simmer the vegetable peelings, covered, for 1 hour. Strain the stock, discarding the peelings; if necessary, reduce the stock to strengthen its flavor. Allow it to cool and store it in the refrigerator or freezer.

## Citrus-based Aspics

Strictly speaking, a "citrus-based" aspic is not an aspic at all. By tradition, if not by definition, aspics are meat-based, having first been made, before the advent of commercially marketed gelatin, from homemade stock so rich in gelatin that no additive was needed to make the recipe set.

The refreshing coolness of lemon-, lime-, and orange-flavored gelatin dishes makes them attractive, neverthless, and they are included to vary the many possibilities already open to the inventive cook who wants to experiment with main-dish aspics.

One word of caution, however: Be careful not to oversweeten them, otherwise they will taste more like desserts than main dishes. True, they should not be sour, but they should be tart.

### Lemon or Lime Aspic

YIELD: ABOUT 1¼ QUARTS
PREPARATION: 25 MINUTES
CHILLING TIME: 6 HOURS

> 1 cup strained fresh lemon *or* lime juice
> 2½ cups water
> Sugar
> A pinch of salt

In a mixing bowl, combine the juice and water; season the mixture to taste.

> 2 envelopes unflavored gelatin, softened for 5 minutes in
> ½ cup cold water

Over simmering water, dissolve the gelatin; add it to the juice, stirring to blend the mixture. Chill the aspic until it just begins to set; add to it the chilled solid ingredient or ingredients of your choice and transfer it to a prepared mold. Chill the aspic for at least 6 hours, or until it is thoroughly set. Unmold it onto a chilled serving plate.

## Orange Aspic

*A stronger orange flavor results from using 2 six-ounce cans frozen orange-juice concentrate plus water to equal 4 cups in place of the fresh juice; in this case, the aspic will not be transparent.*

YIELD: ABOUT 1¼ QUARTS
PREPARATION: 25 MINUTES
CHILLING TIME: 6 HOURS

> 4 cups strained fresh orange juice
> 2 envelopes unflavored gelatin
> A pinch of salt

In ½ cup of the juice, soften the gelatin for 5 minutes. Over simmering water, dissolve the gelatin; add it and the salt to the remaining orange juice, stirring to blend the mixture. Chill the aspic until it just begins to set; add to it the chilled solid ingredient or ingredients of your choice and transfer it to a prepared mold. Chill the aspic for at least 6 hours, or until it is thoroughly set. Unmold it onto a chilled serving plate.

## Tomato Aspic

8 TO 10 SERVINGS
PREPARATION: 30 MINUTES (THE PREPARATION TIME DOES NOT INCLUDE SIMMERING THE VEGETABLES)
CHILLING TIME: 6 HOURS

Lightly oil and chill a 2-quart ring mold or individual molds.

> 4 tablespoons butter
> 3 large ribs celery with their leaves, chopped
> 1 clove garlic, peeled and chopped
> 2 medium-size onions, peeled and chopped

In a soup kettle, heat the butter and in it, over medium heat, cook the celery, garlic, and onion for 10 minutes.

| | |
|---|---|
| 6 medium-size ripe tomatoes, quartered | 2 bay leaves |
| 2½ cups tomato juice | 3 whole cloves |
| Juice and grated rind of 1 medium-size lemon | 1 teaspoon tarragon |
| | 2 teaspoons sugar |
| 1½ tablespoons Worcestershire sauce | 1 teaspoon salt |
| | 8 peppercorns |

To the contents of the soup kettle, add the tomatoes, tomato juice, lemon juice and rind, Worcestershire sauce, bay leaves, cloves, tarragon, and sugar, salt, and peppercorns. Bring the liquid to the boil, reduce the heat, and simmer the mixture, covered, for 45 minutes.

2½ envelopes unflavored gelatin
1 cup tomato juice

In a large mixing bowl, sprinkle the gelatin over the tomato juice and allow it to soften for 5 minutes. Into the gelatin, strain the cooked tomato mixture, forcing through as much vegetable pulp as possible; discard the residue. Stir the mixture to dissolve the gelatin. Allow the aspic to cool; transfer it to the prepared mold, and chill it for at least 6 hours, or until it is thoroughly set. Unmold the aspic onto a chilled serving plate, garnish it with salad greens of your choice, and, if desired, fill the center with a composed salad, pages 193–197.

*Variation:*

If desired, 3 large ribs of celery, diced, blanched for 15 seconds in boiling salted water, and drained, may be stirred into the aspic when it just begins to set. A nice crunchy texture! Fine-chopped parsley, ¼ to ½ cupful, is also a pleasant addition.

When adding solid ingredients to aspic, chill the liquid gelatin in a mixing bowl until it just begins to set. Beat it briefly; stir in the solid ingredients; using a rubber spatula, transfer the mixture to the prepared mold. Complete the recipe as written.

*Make the dish colorful . . .*
If desired, using one or more of the ingredients listed below, make a circle around the bottom of a ring mold or arrange a pattern of your

own design in some other mold. Hold the design in place by pouring over it a little gelatin just on the point of setting; allow this part of the aspic to set before continuing with the recipe.

*Carrots*, scraped and sliced thin
*Chives*, chopped fine
*Cucumber* slices, unpeeled and very thin
*Eggs*, hard-cooked and sliced thin
*Grapes*, seedless, halved lengthwise
*Liver pâté*, cut into attractive shapes
*Mint*, fresh, the leaves arranged in patterns
*Mushrooms*, raw, sliced very thin
*Olives*, black and stuffed, cut into thin rounds
*Parsley*, chopped fine
*Pepper*, sweet green and red, seeded and cut into julienne
   strips
*Pickles*, sweet gherkins, cut into thin rounds
*Pimientos*, cut into julienne strips
*Pineapple* tidbits (canned)
*Radishes*, cut into thin rounds
*Scallions*, cut into thin rounds
*Tarragon*, the fresh leaves arranged in a pattern
*Truffles*, very expensive but very tasty
*Watercress*, the woody stems removed and the tender sprigs
   arranged in an attractive pattern

Having decorated the aspic itself, garnish the serving plate for an attractive presentation. To do so, use:

*Dill weed*, snipped and sprinkled over
*Eggs*, hard-cooked, sliced thin or lengthwise
*Lemon*, sliced thin and seeded
*Lime*, sliced thin and seeded
*Mint*, fresh
*Olives*, black or stuffed, whole *or* cut into rounds
*Orange*, sliced thin and seeded, *or* peeled, sectioned, and seeded
*Parsley*, in sprigs *or* chopped fine
*Pepper*, sweet green or red, seeded and cut into julienne strips
*Radishes*, partially peeled or whole, *or* sliced thin *or* "flow-
   ered" (peel the outer skin back but do not remove it; store
   the radishes for several hours in ice water)

*Tomatoes,* cherry *or* large, thoroughly ripe and very red; cherry
tomatoes may be used whole *or* cut, large tomatoes should
be sliced or sectioned
*Watercress,* the woody stems removed

**ASPARAGUS TIPS IN ASPIC:** Stir in 1½ cupfuls of asparagus tips cooked until just tender, drained, refreshed in cold water, and
drained on absorbent paper. Recommended gelatins: chicken, veal,
vegetable, lemon, orange, tomato.

*Variation:*

Use ¾ cupful of asparagus tips and ¾ cupful of diced cooked chicken.

**AVOCADO IN ASPIC:** Peel, seed, slice lengthwise, and paint
with fresh lemon juice 2 large ripe avocados; with them, line the prepared mold; add the gelatin when it is just about to set. Chill the mold
at once. Recommended gelatins: chicken, veal, vegetable, lemon, lime,
orange.

If desired, 1 cupful of sour cream may be used as part of the liquid
ingredient when making the gelatin and other liquids reduced ac-
cordingly.

*Variations:*

In the container of a food processor or blender, purée the avocados
with 1 cupful  of sour cream and the strained juice of 1 large lime;
use this mixture as part of the liquid ingredient, adding to it strained
fresh orange juice to equal 3½ cupfuls. If desired, add a few drops of
green food coloring.

**AVOCADO WITH CARROT IN ASPIC:** Follow the direc-
tions above, adding to the gelatin ¼ cupful of raisins, plumped in hot
water for 5 minutes and drained on absorbent paper, and 1½ cupfuls
of fine-shredded carrot.

**BEEF IN ASPIC:** Fold in 1½ cupfuls of diced cooked beef.
Recommended gelatins: beef, veal, vegetable, orange, tomato.

**BEETS IN ASPIC:** In a colander, drain and rinse with cold
water 1 one-pound can of shredded beets; drain them on absorbent

paper. Use 1 cup of sour cream as part of the liquid measure in making the gelatin; stir in the beets and 1 teaspoonful of prepared horseradish before transferring the gelatin to the prepared mold. Recommended gelatins: chicken, veal, vegetable, orange.

**BROCCOLI IN ASPIC:** Cook 1 large bunch fresh broccoli for 15 minutes or 2 ten-ounce packages frozen chopped broccoli according to the directions on the package; do not overcook it. Refresh it in cold water; drain it on absorbent paper; chop the fresh broccoli coarse. Peel and chop fine 1 small red onion. Use ½ cupful of Mayonnaise, page 189, as part of the liquid ingredient when making the gelatin. Stir the broccoli and the onion into the gelatin before transferring it to the prepared mold. Recommended gelatins: chicken, veal, lemon, tomato.

**BRUSSELS SPROUTS IN ASPIC:** Trim and rinse 1 pint of Brussels sprouts; in boiling salted water to which are added 2 table-spoonfuls of cider vinegar, cook the sprouts for 10 minutes, or until they are just tender. Refresh them in cold water; drain them on absorbent paper; quarter them. Line the prepared mold with the quartered sprouts and add the aspic when it is just on the point of setting. Chill the mold at once. Recommended gelatins: chicken, veal, vegetable, orange, tomato.

**CABBAGE IN ASPIC:** After dissolving the gelatin, stir in 1 tablespoonful of prepared horseradish. When it is just about to set, stir into the gelatin 2 cupfuls of fine-chopped young cabbage. Recommended gelatins: chicken, vegetable, lemon, tomato.

**CARROTS AND RAISINS IN ASPIC:** Plump ½ cupful of raisins in hot water for 5 minutes; drain them on absorbent paper. Prepare 1 cupful of fine-shredded carrot. Prepare Vinaigrette Sauce, page 191, omitting the olive oil. Toss the raisins and carrot in the sauce and allow it to macerate for 30 minutes; drain the mixture and stir it into the gelatin. Recommended gelatins: veal, vegetable, lemon, orange.

**CHICKEN IN ASPIC:** Stir in 1½ cupfuls of diced cooked chicken. Recommended gelatins: chicken, lemon, lime, orange, tomato.

**CHICKEN SALAD WITH FRUIT IN ASPIC:** Make Chicken Salad, page 195; to it, add 1 eleven-ounce can of mandarin oranges, drained; 1 eight-and-three-ounce can of pineapple tidbits, drained; ½ cupful of toasted slivered almonds; and ¼ cupful of fine-chopped parsley. Blend the mixture well. Make the gelatin with 1½ envelopes unflavored gelatin and 2 cups of liquid. Stir in the chicken mixture. Recommended gelatins: chicken, vegetable, lemon, lime, orange.

CLAMS IN ASPIC: Drain 2 six-ounce cans of minced clams; use the clam juice as part of the liquid ingredient. When the gelatin is just about to set, stir in the reserved clams, ½ cupful of diced celery, and 1 small cucumber, peeled, seeded, and diced. Recommended gelatins: lemon, tomato.

COTTAGE CHEESE IN ASPIC: In a mixing bowl using two forks, toss 1 cupful of dry cottage cheese to separate the curds; stir the curds into the gelatin before transferring it to the prepared mold. Recommended gelatins: all.

CRABMEAT IN ASPIC: Use ½ cupful of Mayonnaise, page 189, and ¼ cupful of chili sauce as part of the liquid ingredient. Stir in 2 six-and-one-half-ounce cans of lump crabmeat, the cartilage removed, and ½ cupful of diced celery. Recommended gelatins: vegetable, lemon, tomato.

CREAM CHEESE IN ASPIC: Roll small balls from 1 eight-ounce and 1 three-ounce package of cream cheese; fold them into the aspic just before transferring it to the prepared mold. Recommended gelatins: all.

CUCUMBER IN ASPIC WITH YOGURT: Peel, seed, and dice 3 medium-size cucumbers; use 2 cupfuls of plain yogurt and one-half of the liquid measure in making the gelatin. Into the gelatin, stir the prepared cucumber and ½ cupful of fine-chopped parsley. Recommended gelatins: lemon, lime, orange.

DATES IN ASPIC WITH ONION: Use 3 tablespoonfuls of malt vinegar as part of the liquid ingredient when making the gelatin; add sugar to the mixture so that it has a sweet-and-pungent flavor. Stir in 1 eight-ounce package pitted dates, chopped, and 1 small Spanish (Bermuda) onion, peeled and chopped fine. Recommended gelatins:

lemon, lime, orange (or make the gelatin with canned pineapple juice as the liquid ingredient).

DEVILED EGGS IN ASPIC: Hard boil, peel, and devil 6 eggs. (Cut the eggs lengthwise, remove the yolks, and, in a mixing bowl, blend them with ¼ cupful of Mayonnaise, page 189, 1 small onion, peeled and grated, 1½ teaspoonfuls of prepared mustard, and ¼ cupful of fine-chopped parsley; season the mixture with salt and pepper to taste, and with it fill the cavities of the reserved egg whites.) Line the prepared mold with the eggs, bottom sides up; add the aspic when it is about to set, and chill the mold at once. Recommended gelatins: chicken, veal, vegetable, tomato.

HARD-COOKED EGGS IN ASPIC: Hard boil, peel, and slice 4 to 6 eggs; with them, line the bottom of the prepared mold; add the setting gelatin and chill the mold at once. Recommended gelatins: beef, chicken, veal, tomato.

FISH IN ASPIC: Stir in 1½ cupfuls of flaked cooked lean fish (cod, flounder, haddock, scrod, sole). Recommended gelatins: chicken, vegetable, lemon, lime, orange, tomato.

HAM IN ASPIC: Stir in 1½ cupfuls of diced cooked ham; add, if desired, ¼ cupful of fine-chopped sweet pickle. Recommended gelatins: chicken, vegetable, tomato.

HAM AND GRAPEFRUIT IN ASPIC: Stir in 1 cupful of diced cooked ham; line the prepared mold with the seeded sections of 1 medium-size grapefruit. Recommended gelatins: chicken, lemon, orange.

HERRING IN ASPIC: Drain and rinse with cold water 1 thirteen-ounce jar of herring in wine sauce; dry the herring on absorbent paper and cut each piece into quarters; stir them and ½ cupful of fine-chopped parsley into the gelatin before transferring it to the prepared mold. Recommended gelatins: lemon, lime, tomato.

KIDNEY BEANS IN ASPIC: Drain and rinse 1 twenty-ounce can of white or red kidney beans; fold them into the gelatin before transferring it to the prepared mold. Recommended gelatins: all (use white or red beans depending upon the color of the gelatin).

**LAMB IN ASPIC:** Stir in 1½ cupfuls of diced cooked lean lamb. Recommended gelatins: beef, chicken, veal, vegetable, orange, tomato.

*Variation:*

Stir in ¾ cupful of diced cooked lamb, ¾ cupful of tenderized pitted prunes, chopped fine, and ¼ cupful of toasted slivered almonds.

**LEEKS IN ASPIC:** In lightly salted boiling water just to cover, cook 6 large leeks, thoroughly rinsed and trimmed, until they are tender; refresh them in cold water; drain them on absorbent paper and chop them coarse, using a little of the green. Use 1 cupful of the leek water as part of the liquid ingredient in making the gelatin. Stir in the prepared leeks before transferring the gelatin to the mold. Recommended gelatins: chicken, veal, vegetable, tomato.

**LENTILS IN ASPIC:** In boiling salted water to cover, cook 2 cupfuls of lentils for 2 minutes; remove them from the heat and allow them to stand, covered, for 1 hour. To them, add 1 small onion stuck with 2 cloves, 1 bay leaf, and 1 teaspoonful of sugar. Bring them to the boil, reduce the heat, and simmer them, covered, for about 45 minutes, or until they are tender but still retain their shape. Discard the onion and bay leaf; refresh the lentils in cold water, and drain them thoroughly. Trim and slice thin 6 scallions. Into the prepared gelatin, stir the lentils, scallions, and ½ cupful of fine-chopped parsley. Recommended gelatins: all.

**LETTUCE IN ASPIC:** Stir in 3 cupfuls of chopped iceberg lettuce. Fill the center of the mold with a composed salad of your choice, pages 193–197. Recommended gelatins: chicken, veal, vegetable, lemon, orange.

**LIVER PÂTÉ IN ASPIC:** Chill 2 four-ounce cans liver pâté. Working rapidly, roll the pâté into small balls; chill them; fold them into the gelatin before transferring it to the prepared mold; add, if desired, ½ cupful of fine-chopped parsley. Recommended gelatins: beef, chicken, veal, tomato.

**SWEET PEPPERS IN ASPIC:** Stir in 2 medium green and 2 medium sweet red peppers, seeded and diced, and ½ cupful of diced celery. Recommended gelatins: chicken, veal, vegetable, orange, tomato.

**RADISHES IN ASPIC WITH SOUR CREAM:** Trim and slice thin 24 radishes; peel and chop fine 1 medium-size red onion. Use 1 cupful of sour cream and 2 tablespoonfuls of red wine vinegar as part of the liquid ingredient when making the gelatin. Into the gelatin, stir the radishes and onion before transferring the mixture to the prepared mold. Recommended gelatins: lemon, orange, tomato.

**SAUERKRAUT IN ASPIC WITH GRAPES:** In 2 cupfuls of dry white wine, cook 1 pound of sauerkraut until it is very tender. Drain thoroughly and chop it fine; allow it to cool and then chill it. Prepare 1 cupful of seedless grapes, halved lengthwise. Into the gelatin, just as it is about to set, stir the chilled sauerkraut and grapes, transfer the mixture to the prepared mold. Recommended gelatins: chicken, veal, vegetable, orange, tomato.

**SCALLOPS IN ASPIC:** Cook ¾ of a pound of sea scallops in a minimum of water until they are tender but still firm. Drain, reserving the liquid; quarter them; allow them to cool and then chill them. Use the reserved liquid as part of the liquid ingredient when making the gelatin. Stir in the prepared scallops and ¼ cupful of fine-chopped parsley. Recommended gelatins: lemon, orange, tomato.

**SHRIMP IN ASPIC:** Stir in 1½ cupfuls of coarse-chopped cooked shrimp. Recommended gelatins: lemon, lime, orange, tomato.

**SHRIMP SALAD IN ASPIC:** Make Shrimp Salad, page 195; fold in ½ cupful of heavy cream, whipped. Make the gelatin with 1½ envelopes of unflavored gelatin and 2 cupfuls of liquid. Fold in the shrimp mixture when the gelatin is just about to set. Recommended gelatins: chicken, vegetable, lemon, lime, orange.

**SPINACH IN ASPIC WITH HORSERADISH:** In boiling salted water, wilt 2 ten-ounce packages fresh spinach or cook 2 ten-ounce packages of frozen chopped spinach according to the directions on the package. Press it dry in a sieve; chop the fresh spinach fine; stir it into the gelatin, together with 1½ teaspoonfuls of prepared horse-radish (or more, to taste). Recommended gelatins: chicken, veal, vege-table, lemon, orange.

SWEETBREADS IN ASPIC: Prepare and chill 1 pound of sweetbreads, page 15. Prepare the sections from 1 large grapefruit and 1 cupful of diced celery. Prepare 2 cupfuls of gelatin. Into the prepared mold, pour one-quarter of the gelatin and chill it until it is just set. Over the gelatin, arrange in layers the sweetbreads, celery, and grape-fruit sections. Meanwhile, chill the remaining gelatin until it is syrupy; pour it over the contents of the mold and chill the aspic for at least 6 hours, or until it is thoroughly set. Recommended gelatins: chicken, veal, vegetable, lemon, orange.

*Variations:*

VARIATION I: Substitute 3 medium-size cucumbers, peeled, seeded, and diced, for the celery.

VARIATION II: Fold ½ cupful of heavy cream, whipped, into the gelatin just before it is poured the second time.

TONGUE IN ASPIC: Stir in 1½ cupfuls of diced cooked tongue; add, if desired, ¼ cupful of fine-chopped sweet pickle. Recom-mended gelatins: beef, chicken, veal, vegetable, orange, tomato.

TUNA IN ASPIC: Stir in 1 seven-ounce can of water-pack tuna, drained and flaked; 1 small onion, peeled and chopped fine; ½ cupful of diced celery; and ½ cupful of fine-shredded carrot. Recommended gelatins: lemon, tomato.

TUNA IN ASPIC WITH FRUIT: Using 1½ envelopes of unflavored gelatin, make one-half the quantity of gelatin. When it is just about to set, stir in 1 seven-ounce can of water-pack tuna, drained and flaked; the seeded sections of 1 small orange or tangerine; ½ cupful of golden raisins, plumped for 5 minutes in hot water and thoroughly drained; and 1 large tart apple, peeled, cored, and diced. Recommended gelatins: lemon, tomato.

**TURKEY IN ASPIC:** Stir in 1½ cupfuls of diced cooked turkey. Recommended gelatins: chicken, vegetable, orange, tomato.

**TURKEY SALAD IN ASPIC:** Make Turkey Salad, page 195. Make the gelatin with 1½ envelopes of unflavored gelatin and 2 cups of liquid. Stir in the Turkey Salad. Recommended gelatins: chicken, vegetable, lemon, lime, orange.

**VEAL IN ASPIC:** Use ½ cupful of Mayonnaise, page 189, as part of the liquid ingredient when making the gelatin. Stir in 1 cupful of diced cooked lean veal, ¼ cupful of diced celery, and 1 small onion, peeled and chopped fine; if desired, add ¼ cupful of toasted slivered almonds. If available, season the mixture with 1 teaspoonful of fine-chopped fresh tarragon. Recommended gelatins: chicken, veal, vegetable, orange.

**MIXED COOKED VEGETABLES IN ASPIC:** Cook 2 ten-ounce packages of frozen mixed vegetables according to the directions on the package; do not overcook them. Refresh the vegetables in cold water; drain them on absorbent paper and stir them into the gelatin before transferring it to the prepared mold. Recommended gelatins: all.

**MIXED RAW VEGETABLES IN ASPIC:** Stir in 2 medium-size cucumbers, peeled, seeded, and diced; 1 small red onion, peeled and chopped fine; 1 green and 1 sweet red pepper, seeded and diced; 3 medium-size ripe tomatoes, peeled, seeded, chopped, and drained; ¼ cupful of fine-chopped parsley; and the strained juice of 1 medium lemon. Recommended gelatins: lemon, lime, orange, tomato.

*Variation:*

In place of the vegetables listed above, use: 1 cupful of fine-grated cabbage; ½ cupful of fine-grated carrot; ½ cupful of fine-chopped celery; ¾ cupful of cooked green peas (*or* of uncooked frozen tiny peas, fully thawed to room temperature); ⅓ cupful of thin-sliced radish; and 2 medium-size ripe tomatoes, peeled, seeded, and chopped.

WATERCRESS AND WATER CHESTNUTS IN ASPIC:
Discard the woody stems from 1 bunch of watercress; rinse, drain on
absorbent paper, and chop the leaves. Drain 1 five-ounce can of water
chestnuts and slice them thin. Stir the watercress and water chestnuts
into the gelatin before transferring it to the prepared mold. Recommended gelatins: chicken, veal, vegetable, lemon, orange.

*Variation:*

Use only watercress and increase the quantity to 2 bunches.

## Jellied Baba Ghanouge

6 SERVINGS

PREPARATION: 25 MINUTES (THE PREPARATION TIME DOES NOT INCLUDE
    COOKING THE EGGPLANT)

CHILLING TIME: 6 HOURS

Lightly oil and chill a 5-cup ring or other mold.

**1 large eggplant**

With the tines of a fork, pierce the eggplant in several places. Place it
on a baking sheet and cook it in a 400° oven for 40 minutes, or until
it is very soft. Skin the eggplant and put the pulp in the container of a
food processor or blender.

**5 tablespoons *tahine***         **Juice and grated rind of**
  **(sesame-seed purée,**             **1 medium-size lemon**
  **available at specialty and**    **1 teaspoon salt**
  **health-food stores)**          **½ teaspoon pepper**
**1 teaspoon prepared horse-**
  **radish**

To the contents of the container, add the *tahine,* horseradish, lemon
juice and rind, and seasonings. Whirl the mixture until it is smooth.
Chill the *baba ghanouge.*

   Using 2 envelopes of unflavored gelatin, make one-half the Lemon
Aspic recipe, page 118. When it is just about to set, fold in the chilled
*baba ghanouge;* transfer the mixture to the prepared mold and chill it
for at least 6 hours, or until it is thoroughly set. Unmold it onto a
chilled serving plate.

## Cranberries in Aspic

6 SERVINGS
PREPARATION: 45 MINUTES
CHILLING TIME: 6 HOURS

Lightly oil and chill a 5-cup ring mold

    1 pound cranberries, rinsed          ½ teaspoon salt
    1 cup sugar                            2 cups water
    2 three-inch pieces cinnamon
       stick and 12 cloves, tied
       in cheesecloth

In a saucepan, combine the cranberries, sugar, spices, salt, and water. Bring the liquid to the boil, reduce the heat, and cook the cranberries, stirring to dissolve the sugar, until they have burst and are tender.

    2 envelopes unflavored gelatin, softened for 5 minutes in
       ½ cup of strained orange juice
    1 eight-ounce can of crushed pineapple, with its liquid

Into the hot cranberries, stir the gelatin; when it is dissolved, stir in the pineapple. Allow the mixture to cool before transferring it to the prepared mold. Chill the aspic for at least 6 hours, or until it is thoroughly set. Unmold it onto a chilled serving plate.

## Cucumber Aspic

6 TO 8 SERVINGS
PREPARATION: 45 MINUTES
CHILLING TIME: 6 HOURS

Lightly oil and chill a 5-cup ring or other mold.

    4 medium cucumbers, peeled, seeded, and chopped
    2 cups water
    1 teaspoon salt

In a saucepan, cook the cucumbers in the salted water, covered, for 20 minutes, or until they are mushy. In the container of a food processor or blender, whirl them with their water until the mixture is smooth.

> 2 envelopes unflavored gelatin, softened for 5 minutes in ½
> cup of cold water

To the contents of the container, add the softened gelatin and whirl the mixture until the gelatin is dissolved. Transfer the mixture to a mixing bowl.

> 1 small onion, peeled and grated
> Strained juice of 1 small lemon
> 1 teaspoon Worcestershire sauce
> A drop or 2 of Tabasco sauce
> A drop or 2 of green food coloring (optional)

Stir in the onion, lemon juice, seasonings, and food coloring. Allow the mixture to cool, pour it into the prepared mold, and chill it for at least 6 hours, or until it is thoroughly set. Unmold it onto a chilled serving plate.

*Variation:*

C U C U M B E R   A S P I C   W I T H   C A V I A R :   Line the bottom of the prepared mold with salmon roe caviar (a 3-ounce jar spread evenly over the bottom of the mold should be adequate); chill the mold. Prepare the recipe for Cucumber Aspic (above), and, when it is just about to set, transfer it to the mold; chill the mold at once.

## Eggs in Tarragon Aspic

6 SERVINGS
PREPARATION: 35 MINUTES
CHILLING TIME: 6 HOURS

Lightly oil and chill 6 custard cups.

> 2 cups chicken, veal, *or*
> vegetable stock
> 1 envelope plus 1 teaspoon
> unflavored gelatin,
> softened for 5 minutes
> in ¼ cup of cold water
>
> 1 tablespoon fresh
> tarragon leaves,
> bruised *or* 2
> teaspoons dried
> tarragon
> Salt

In a saucepan, bring the stock to the boil; add the gelatin and tarragon, stirring until the gelatin is dissolved. Remove the saucepan from the heat, cover it, and allow the tarragon to infuse for 30 minutes. Adjust the seasoning to taste.

**6 small eggs**

Meanwhile, poach the eggs in acidulated water *or* boil them for 4 or 5 minutes. Remove the poached eggs to absorbent paper. Immerse the boiled eggs in cold water and peel them. Reserve the eggs.

**2 tablespoons Madeira *or* dry sherry**

Into the cooled gelatin, stir the wine of your choice.

**12 leaves fresh tarragon *or* 6 leaves parsley**

In 6 four-ounce custard cups, arrange the tarragon leaves, crossed. Over the leaves, strain about ½ inch of gelatin. Chill the cups until the gelatin is nearly set.

**Reserved eggs**

In each cup, arrange an egg. Strain the remaining gelatin equally into the dishes. Chill them for at least 6 hours, or until the aspic is thoroughly set. To serve, unmold the individual aspics onto chilled plates.

## Guacamole in Aspic

8 SERVINGS
PREPARATION: 30 MINUTES
CHILLING TIME: 6 HOURS

Lightly oil and chill a 5-cup ring mold.

| | |
|---|---|
| 3 large ripe avocados, peeled, seeded, and chopped coarse | 2 tablespoons lemon juice |
| | ¾ teaspoon chili powder |
| | A few drops of Tabasco sauce |
| 1 small onion, peeled and chopped coarse | ½ teaspoon sugar |
| 1 clove garlic, put through a press | ¾ teaspoon salt |

In the container of a food processor or blender, combine the avocado, onion, garlic, lemon juice, chili powder, and remaining seasonings. Whirl the mixture until it is smooth. Transfer it to a mixing bowl.

**1 large ripe tomato, peeled, seeded, and chopped**

Into the avocado mixture, fold the tomato. Chill the *guacamole*.

Using 2 envelopes of unflavored gelatin, make one-half the Lemon Aspic recipe, page 118. When it is just about to set, fold in the chilled *guacamole*; transfer the mixture to the prepared mold and chill it for at least 6 hours, or until it is thoroughly set. Unmold it onto a bed of chilled salad greens.

## Oysters in Aspic

6 SERVINGS
PREPARATION: 50 MINUTES
CHILLING TIME: 6 HOURS

Lightly oil and chill a 5-cup ring mold.

**1 pound small mushrooms, wiped clean with a damp cloth
    and sliced
½ cup dry white wine
½ cup light cream**

In a skillet or saucepan, combine the mushrooms, white wine, and cream. Bring the liquid to the boil, reduce the heat, and simmer the mushrooms, covered, until they are tender but still hold their shape. Reserve both mushrooms and liquid.

| | |
|---|---|
| **2 tablespoons butter** | **1 cup milk** |
| **2 tablespoons flour** | **Salt** |
| **A generous grating of nutmeg** | **White pepper** |

In a saucepan, heat the butter and in it, over gentle heat, cook the flour for a few minutes. Stir in the nutmeg. Gradually add the milk, stirring constantly until the mixture is thickened and smooth. Season the *béchamel* with salt and pepper to taste.

24 to 30 stewing oysters, with their juice
½ cup dry white wine
1½ envelopes unflavored gelatin, softened for 5 minutes in
        ¼ cup cold water

In a saucepan, combine the oysters and wine. Over gentle heat, cook
the oysters until their edges just begin to curl. Remove the saucepan
from the heat and add the gelatin, stirring until it is dissolved.

### Reserved mushrooms and mushroom liquid

In a mixing bowl, combine the mushrooms and their liquid with the
*béchamel*; stir the mixture gently to blend it well without breaking the
mushrooms. Add the oysters and their liquid, once again stirring gently
to blend the mixture well. Allow it to cool. Transfer the mixture to
the prepared mold and chill it for at least 6 hours, or until it is thoroughly set. Unmold the aspic onto a chilled serving plate.

## Seviche in Aspic

6 SERVINGS
PREPARATION: 30 MINUTES (THE PREPARATION TIME DOES NOT INCLUDE
    MARINATING THE FISH)
CHILLING TIME: 6 HOURS

Lightly oil and chill a 6-cup ring or other mold.

2 cups fresh strained lime
    juice *or* 1 cup strained
    lime juice mixed with 1
    cup fresh strained lemon
    juice
2 medium red onions, peeled
    and chopped fine

1 clove garlic, put
    through a press
1 teaspoon chili powder
1 teaspoon salt

In a mixing bowl, combine and blend the juice, onion, garlic, chili
powder, and salt.

1½ pounds raw flounder filet, cut into ½-inch pieces

In a flat glass or ceramic dish, arrange the fish pieces in an even layer.
Over them, pour the juice mixture so that the fish is covered by the

marinade. Cover the dish and refrigerate it for at least 3 hours. When the fish is white and opaque, it is ready to eat.

With a slotted spoon, remove the fish pieces from the marinade. Reserve both the fish and the marinade.

> 2 envelopes unflavored gelatin, softened for 5 minutes in
>    ½ cup cold water

Over simmering water, dissolve the gelatin and reserve it.

> Reserved marinade
> 1¼ cups water
> Sugar
> Reserved fish

To the marinade, add 1¼ cups water and sugar to taste (the marinade should not be sweet). Stir in the dissolved gelatin. Chill the mixture until it just begins to set. Stir in the reserved fish, transfer the aspic to the prepared mold and chill it for at least 6 hours, or until it is thoroughly set. Unmold it onto a chilled serving plate.

## Split Pea Aspic with Mint

8 SERVINGS

PREPARATION: 30 MINUTES (THE PREPARATION TIME DOES NOT INCLUDE
   COOKING THE SPLIT PEAS)
CHILLING TIME: 6 HOURS

Lightly oil and chill a 6-cup ring mold.

> 3½ cups chicken stock, boiling
> 1 cup split green peas

Add the split peas to the boiling chicken stock; remove the saucepan from the heat, cover it, and allow the peas to stand for 1 hour. Return the saucepan to the stove.

> 1 medium-size onion, peeled and chopped coarse
> 1 large rib celery with its leaves, chopped coarse
> 1 bay leaf
> 1 cup fresh mint leaves
> 1 teaspoon salt

To the contents of the saucepan, add the onion, celery, bay leaf, mint leaves, and salt. Bring the liquid to the boil, reduce the heat, and simmer the peas, covered, for 1 hour, or until they are very tender and start to disintegrate. Remove the bay leaf.

> 2 envelopes plus 1 teaspoon unflavored gelatin, softened for
> 5 minutes in ½ cup cold water

To the contents of the saucepan, add the gelatin, stirring to dissolve it. Allow the mixture to cool.

In the container of a food processor or blender, whirl the mixture, two cupfuls at a time, until it is smooth.

> Strained juice of 1 small lemon
> A few drops of Tabasco sauce
> Salt

Add the lemon juice and Tabasco sauce, and adjust the seasoning with salt to taste. Whirl the mixture briefly once more before transferring it to a mixing bowl. Chill the mixture until it just begins to set.

> ½ cup heavy cream, whipped

Beat the mixture briefly to eliminate any lumps; fold in the whipped cream. Using a rubber spatula, transfer the aspic to the prepared mold and chill it for at least 6 hours, or until it is thoroughly set.

> Mixed Vegetable Salad, page 197

Unmold the aspic onto a chilled serving plate; fill the center with some of the salad and offer the remainder separately.

## Tripe in Aspic

8 TO 10 SERVINGS
PREPARATION: 20 MINUTES
COOKING: 1½ HOURS
CHILLING TIME: 6 HOURS

*An appetizer at dinner or a main course at luncheon*

Lightly oil and chill an 8-inch loaf pan

1 pound honeycomb tripe,
    cut into ½-inch dice
3 cups water
2 bay leaves

3 whole cloves
8 peppercorns
1½ teaspoons salt

In a saucepan, combine the tripe, water, and seasonings. Bring the liquid to the boil, reduce the heat, and simmer the tripe for 1 hour. Discard the bay leaves, cloves, and peppercorns.

6 medium-size carrots, scraped and sliced thin
2 medium-size onions, peeled and chopped fine
2 cloves garlic, peeled and chopped fine

To the contents of the saucepan, add the carrots, onions, and garlic; continue simmering the tripe for 30 minutes, or until it is very tender.

2 envelopes unflavored gelatin, softened in ½ cup cold water
Strained juice of 1 medium-size lemon
½ cup fine-chopped parsley
A few drops of Tabasco sauce
1 tablespoon Worcestershire sauce

To the contents of the saucepan, add the softened gelatin, lemon juice, parsley, and seasonings, stirring until the gelatin is dissolved. Transfer the mixture to the prepared pan, and chill the aspic for at least 6 hours, or until it is thoroughly set.

Vinaigrette Sauce, page 191
Salad greens of your choice

Arrange the greens on a serving plate and unmold the aspic over them; offer the sauce separately.

# Gelatin Desserts

---

Gelatin desserts are very easy to make; they are attractive to look at, pleasing to the palate, and consoling to the calorie-counter. They are a boon to the cook who, having prepared ahead, wants to relax over the meal in sure knowledge that dessert will be successful.

Many different gelatin desserts, like many different soufflés, mousses, aspics, and creams, may be made from a basic recipe. It is only necessary to remember that:

1. 1 envelope of unflavored gelatin will jell 2 cupfuls of liquid ingredient
2. Purée is a liquid ingredient
3. Yogurt is a liquid ingredient (1 cupful of yogurt used in place of 1 cupful of another liquid ingredient yields a smooth and unusually tasty *Pudding*)
4. 2 or 3 egg whites, beaten until stiff but not dry with 2 or 3 tablespoonfuls of sugar and folded into the gelatin, which has been briefly whipped when it is just about to set, will not affect the jelling of the dessert, but will make it much lighter —as with the so-called *Snow* desserts: Apricot Snow, Lemon Snow, and so forth.

With these facts in mind, let us proceed to:

## Basic Dessert Gelatin

4 SERVINGS (THE RECIPE MAY BE DOUBLED)

PREPARATION: ABOUT 15 MINUTES (THE PREPARATION WILL VARY DE-
PENDNG UPON THE INGREDIENTS USED AND THE TIME REQUIRED TO
READY THEM)

CHILLING TIME: 6 HOURS

Lightly oil and chill a 5-cup ring or other mold; or chill a serving dish
or individual dessert glasses.

>    1 envelope unflavored gelatin, softened for 5 minutes in ¼
>        cup cold water or fruit juice

Over simmering water, dissolve the gelatin and reserve it.

>    2 cups liquid ingredient
>    Sugar, as called for
>    Special seasonings, as called for
>    A pinch of salt
>    Reserved gelatin

In a mixing bowl, combine the liquid ingredient, sugar, special seasonings, salt, and reserved gelatin; stir the mixture until the sugar is dissolved. Chill it until it just begins to set.

>    1 to 1½ cups solid ingredient, as called for or desired (any
>        prepared fruit)
>    2 or 3 egg whites, beaten until stiff but not dry with 2 or 3
>        tablespoons sugar (optional)

Briefly whip the chilled gelatin and then fold in the solid ingredient.
(If you want a snow-type dessert, fold in the egg white.) Transfer the
mixture to the prepared mold or dish and chill it for at least 6 hours,
or until it is thoroughly set.

>    Dessert sauce of your choice, pages 191–193 (optional)

Unmold the dessert onto a chilled serving plate or serve it from its dish.
If desired, offer separately the sauce of your choice.

Although a single quantity of this recipe will not fill a 5-cup ring
mold, that container is nonetheless suggested because it will enable

you to fill the center with a fruit of your choice—a very attractive presentation; if the recipe is doubled, as it should be for 6 servings, it will fill the mold adequately.

APRICOT GELATIN: As the liquid ingredient, use 2 cupfuls of seasoned apricot purée; to it, add 1 or 2 drops of almond extract. Recommended also for Pudding and Snow.

CHERRY GELATIN: Drain and reserve the liquid from 1 one-pound can of pitted dark sweet cherries; chop the cherries coarse and reserve them. As the liquid ingredient, use the cherry liquid, ½ cupful of sweet sherry or port wine, the strained juice of 1 medium-size lemon, and water to equal 2 cupfuls; add 2 or 3 drops of almond extract. Fold in the reserved cherries as directed. Recommended also for Snow.

FRESH FRUIT IN GELATIN: Use a 5-cup ring mold; in it, arrange a layer of fresh orange sections, seeded; give the layer an "accent" by continuing the design with ½ cupful of seedless grapes, cut lengthwise. Over the fruit, pour sufficient fruit gelatin of your choice just to cover; chill this layer until it is nearly set; over the set layer, arrange the dice cut from 1 large ripe pear, peeled and cored. Add the remaining gelatin and chill the mold as directed.

GINGER GELATIN (8 SERVINGS): Use 2 envelopes of unflavored gelatin softened in ½ cupful of cold water; as the liquid ingredient, use 1 twelve-ounce jar ginger marmalade, 1 cupful of dry white wine, and 1½ cupfuls of water. Add to the gelatin mixture ½ cupful of fine-chopped crystallized ginger, the strained juice of 1 medium-size lemon, and ½ teaspoonful of vanilla extract. Recommended also for Pudding (use 1 cupful of plain yogurt and ½ cupful of water).

GUAVA GELATIN: As the liquid ingredient, use 1 one-pound can of guava shells and their liquid, puréed in the container of a food processor or blender, plus dry white wine to equal 2 cupfuls; add along with it the juice and grated rind of 1 medium-size lemon; sweeten the mixture with sugar, to taste. Recommended also for Pudding and Snow.

KADOTA FIG GELATIN: As the liquid ingredient, use 1 one-pound can of Kadota figs and their liquid, puréed in the container of a food processor or blender, plus orange juice to equal 2 cupfuls; add to the liquid the juice and grated rind of 1 medium-size lemon. Recommended also for Pudding and Snow.

KUMQUAT GELATIN ( 6 SERVINGS ): Use 1½ envelopes of unflavored gelatin, softened in ½ cupful of orange juice; as the liquid ingredient, use 2 cupfuls of kumquat purée, page 197, and 1 six-ounce container frozen orange juice concentrate plus ¾ cupful of water. Add a few drops of almond extract and, if desired, sweeten the mixture with sugar to taste. Recommended also for Pudding.

LEMON GELATIN: As the liquid ingredient, use ¾ cupful of strained fresh lemon juice and 1 cupful of water. Sweeten the mixture with sugar to taste; add to the liquid ½ teaspoonful of vanilla extract. Recommended also for Pudding and Snow.

LIME GELATIN: As the liquid ingredient, use ½ cupful of strained fresh lime juice and 1½ cupfuls of water. Use ½ cupful of sugar and the grated rind of 1 large lime; add a few drops of green food coloring, if desired. Recommended also for Snow.

LITCHIS AND LOQUATS IN GELATIN: Drain, reserving the liquid, 1 one-pound can each of litchis (lichees) and loquats; to their liquid, add the strained juice of 1 small lemon and water to equal 2 cupfuls; use this mixture as the liquid ingredient. Sweeten the gelatin with sugar to taste. Before transferring it to the prepared mold, fold in the litchis and loquats and 3 tablespoonfuls of fine-chopped crystallized ginger.

MANGO GELATIN: As the liquid ingredient, use 1 one-pound can of sliced mango and its liquid, puréed in the container of a food processor or blender, plus strained fresh orange juice to equal 2 cupfuls; add 1 tablespoonful of rose water or 3 drops of almond extract. Recommended also for Pudding.

MELON GELATIN: As the liquid ingredient, use the seeded flesh of 1 large ripe cantaloupe or honeydew melon, puréed in the container of a food processor or blender; if necessary, add dry white wine to equal 2 cupfuls. Add the juice of 1 small lemon and sweeten the mixture with sugar to taste. Recommended also for Pudding and Snow.

**MINCEMEAT GELATIN:** As the liquid ingredient, use 1½ cupfuls of prepared mincemeat, ½ cupful of cognac *or* light rum, the juice of 1 large lemon, and water to equal 2 cupfuls; if necessary, add sugar to taste. Recommended also for Pudding.

**FRESH MINT GELATIN:** Over ½ packed cupful of fresh mint leaves, pour 1½ cupfuls of boiling water; allow the leaves to infuse, covered, for 30 minutes. Strain the mixture, reserving the water and discarding the mint leaves; to the mint water, add dry white wine to equal 2 cupfuls; add the strained juice of 1 small lemon, a few drops of green food coloring, and sweeten the mixture with sugar to taste. Before transferring the chilled mixture to the mold, fold in a few fine-chopped mint leaves. Recommended also for Pudding and Snow.

**ORANGE GELATIN:** As the liquid ingredient, use 2 cupfuls of strained fresh orange juice and the strained juice of 1 medium-size lemon; sweeten the mixture with sugar to taste. Recommended also for Pudding and Snow.

**ORANGE GELATIN WITH BANANAS:** Follow the directions for Orange Gelatin (above); line the prepared mold with thin-sliced rounds of ripe banana. Over them pour sufficient gelatin just to cover; chill the mold until this layer is set but still soft. Pour the remaining gelatin into the mold and complete the recipe as written.

**PAPAYA GELATIN:** As the liquid ingredient, use 1 one-pound can of sliced papaya and its liquid, puréed in the container of a food processor or blender, plus strained fresh orange juice to equal 2 cupfuls; add 2 or 3 drops of almond extract. Recommended also for Pudding and Snow.

**PEACH GELATIN:** As the liquid ingredient, use 2 cupfuls of purée made from fresh ripe peaches (prepared in the container of a food processor or blender) mixed with the strained juice of 1 small lemon; add 2 or 3 drops of almond extract. Recommended also for Pudding and Snow.

PEAR GELATIN: As the liquid ingredient, use 2 cupfuls of purée made from fresh ripe pears (prepared in the container of a food processor or blender) mixed with the strained juice of 1 small lemon; add ½ teaspoonful of vanilla extract. Recommended also for Pudding and Snow.

PERSIMMON GELATIN: As the liquid ingredient, use 2 cupfuls of purée made by sieving the pulp of very ripe persimmons; add the strained juice of 1 small lemon and ½ teaspoonful of vanilla extract. Recommended also for Pudding and Snow.

PLUMS IN GELATIN: In the bottom of the mold arrange, skin side down, 2½ cupfuls of fresh ripe plum slices. Over them, pour sufficient Orange Gelatin, page 143, just to cover; chill the gelatin until it is set but still soft; add the remaining gelatin and chill the dessert as directed.

PORT WINE GELATIN: Use 2 envelopes unflavored gelatin, softened for 5 minutes in ⅓ cupful of water; as the liquid ingredient, use 2 cupfuls of dark ruby port, 1 cupful of water, and the strained juices of 1 medium-size lemon and 1 medium-size orange. Sweeten to taste with ½ to ⅔ cupfuls of sugar.
A delicious gelatin to use with a prepared fresh fruit of your choice as the solid ingredient.

PRUNE GELATIN: As the liquid ingredient, use 1 one-pound jar of pitted stewed prunes, puréed with their liquid in the container of a food processor or blender; add the strained juice of 1 medium-size lemon, 2 or 3 drops of almond extract, and water, if necessary, to equal 2 cupfuls. Recommended also for Pudding and Snow.

QUINCE GELATIN: As the liquid ingredient, use 1 one-pound can of quinces and their liquid, puréed in the container of a food processor or blender, plus strained fresh orange juice to equal 2 cupfuls; add 1 tablespoonful of rose water or 2 or 3 drops of almond extract. Recommended also for Pudding and Snow.

RHUBARB GELATIN: As the liquid ingredient, use 2 cupfuls of seasoned stewed rhubarb and the strained juice of 1 small lemon;

add ½ teaspoonful of vanilla extract. Recommended also for Pudding and Snow.

STRAWBERRY GELATIN: As the liquid ingredient, use 1 quart of strawberries, hulled, rinsed, and puréed in the container of a fool processor or blender, plus strained fresh orange juice to equal 2 cupfuls. Sweeten the purée with sugar to taste; add ½ teaspoonful of vanilla extract. Recommended also for Pudding and Snow.

TANGERINE GELATIN: Follow the directions for Orange Gelatin, page 143, substituting fresh strained tangerine juice for the orange juice. Recommended also for Pudding and Snow.

## Avocado Ring

6 TO 8 SERVINGS
PREPARATION: 30 MINUTES
CHILLING TIME: 6 HOURS

Lightly oil and chill a 5-cup ring mold.

    ½ cup cold water
    2 envelopes unflavored gelatin
    ¼ cup sugar
    ½ teaspoon salt
    1½ cups boiling water

Into a mixing bowl, measure the cold water; over it, sprinkle the gelatin and allow it to soften for 5 minutes. Add the sugar, salt, and boiling water, stirring to dissolve the gelatin and sugar.

    2 large ripe avocados, peeled, seeded, chopped coarse, and
        puréed in the container of a food processor or blender
    Strained juice and grated rind of 1 medium-size lemon

Stir in the avocado purée, lemon juice and rind. Transfer the mixture to the prepared mold and chill it for at least 6 hours, or until it is thoroughly set.

    Berries or cut fresh fruit of your choice

Unmold the avocado ring onto a chilled serving plate, fill the center with some of the berries or fruit, and offer the remainder separately.

## Banana and Yogurt Pudding

4 SERVINGS
PREPARATION: 15 MINUTES
CHILLING TIME: 6 HOURS

Lightly oil and chill individual dishes or a 4-cup mold of your choice.

    1 envelope unflavored gelatin
    ¼ cup strained fresh orange juice

Soften the gelatin in the orange juice for 5 minutes and then dissolve it over simmering water.

    2 large very ripe bananas,          A pinch of salt
       peeled and cut up                ¼ teaspoon almond
    1 cup plain yogurt                     extract or ½
    ¾ cup strained fresh orange            teaspoon vanilla
       juice                               extract (optional)
    ¼ cup sugar

In the container of an electric blender, combine the bananas, yogurt, orange juice, sugar, salt, and extract; whirl the ingredients until the mixture is smooth. With the motor running, add the dissolved gelatin.

   Into the prepared dishes or mold, pour the pudding. Chill it for at least 6 hours, or until it is thoroughly set.

    *Crème anglaise*, page 192 (optional)

Onto chilled dessert plates or a serving platter, unmold the pudding. Pass the sauce separately.

*Variation:*

   APPLE (OR PRUNE) AND YOGURT PUDDING: 6 servings. Use 1½ envelopes unflavored gelatin, soften in ½ cup orange juice for 5 minutes and dissolved over simmering water. While the gelatin is softening and dissolving, combine in the container of an electric blender, 1½ cups orange juice, 1 cup apple *or* prune butter, 1 cup plain yogurt, a pinch of salt, and a few drops of almond extract. Whirl the mixture until it is thoroughly blended, then, with the motor running, add the dissolved gelatin. Pour the mixture into individual dishes or a 5-cup mold. Chill the dessert for at least 6 hours, or until it is thoroughly set.

## Grapes in White Wine Gelatin

6 SERVINGS
PREPARATION: 30 MINUTES
CHILLING TIME: 6 HOURS

Chill a 5-cup ring or other mold.

> 2 envelopes unflavored gelatin, softened for 5 minutes in ¼ cup cold water
> 1 cup boiling water
> ½ cup sugar

In a mixing bowl, combine the softened gelatin, boiling water, and sugar, stirring until the gelatin and sugar are dissolved.

> 1 cup dry white wine
> Strained juice of 1 small lemon

Stir in the wine and lemon juice. Allow the mixture to cool and then chill it until it is just about to set.

> 1 cup seedless grapes, rinsed, drained, and halved lengthwise

Fold in the grapes. Transfer the mixture to the mold and chill it for at least 6 hours, or until it is thoroughly set.

> *Crème anglaise*, page 192

Unmold the dessert onto a chilled plate and offer the sauce separately.

*Variation:*

PLUMS IN RED WINE GELATIN: Follow the recipe above, using dry red wine in place of the white, and 12 ripe plums, rinsed, halved lengthwise, and seeded in place of the grapes; arrange the plums in a pattern in the mold, add the gelatin when it is about to set, and chill the dessert at once.

## Lime-and-Mint Gelatin Ring

6 TO 8 SERVINGS

PREPARATION: 35 MINUTES (THE PREPARATION TIME DOES NOT INCLUDE INFUSING THE MINT)

CHILLING TIME: 6 HOURS

Lightly oil and chill a 5-cup ring mold.

> **2 envelopes unflavored gelatin**
> **1 cup cold water**

In a mixing bowl, sprinkle the gelatin over the water and allow it to soften for 5 minutes.

> **⅓ cup, packed, fresh mint leaves, chopped coarse**
> **2 cups boiling water**

To the gelatin, add the mint leaves and boiling water, stirring to dissolve the gelatin. Cover the bowl and allow the mint to infuse for 30 minutes.

> **1 cup sugar**
> **A pinch of salt**
> **A few drops green food coloring**

Add the sugar, salt, and food coloring, stirring to dissolve the sugar.

> **1 cup lime juice**

Stir in the lime juice. Strain the mixture into the prepared mold and chill it for at least 6 hours, or until it is thoroughly set.

> **Berries of your choice *or* melon balls**
> ***Crème anglaise*, page 192 (optional)**

Unmold the dessert onto a chilled plate and fill the center with the fruit of your choice; offer the sauce separately.

## *Rose-water Milk Jelly*

4 TO 6 SERVINGS
PREPARATION: 25 MINUTES
CHILLING TIME: 6 HOURS

*Known in Turkey as* mahallebi, *this exotic dessert, light and delicate, derives its special flavor from rose water, available at Middle Eastern and specialty food stores.*

Chill a 4-cup serving bowl or individual dessert glasses.

> **1 envelope unflavored gelatin, softened for 5 minutes in ¼ cup cold water**

Over simmering water, dissolve the gelatin and reserve it.

> **2 cups milk**
> **¼ cup sugar**
> **A pinch of salt**

In a mixing bowl, combine the milk, sugar, and salt, stirring until the sugar is dissolved.

> **¼ cup rose water**
> **Reserved gelatin**

Add the rose water and gelatin, stirring to blend the ingredients well. Pour the mixture into a serving bowl or individual glasses. Chill it for at least 6 hours, or until it is thoroughly set.

> **Granulated sugar ( optional )**

When serving the dessert, offer the sugar separately.

*Variations:*

ALMOND MILK JELLY: In place of the rose water, use ½ cupful of crushed toasted almonds and ½ teaspoonful of almond extract.

COCONUT MILK JELLY: In place of the rose water, use 1 four-ounce can of flaked coconut; in place of 1 cupful of the milk, use 1 cup of sweetened coconut cream; omit the sugar entirely.

**P I S T A C H I O  M I L K  J E L L Y :** In place of the rose water, use 1 teaspoonful of vanilla extract and add ½ cupful of crushed pistachio nuts when the gelatin is just about to set.

**O R A N G E - W A T E R  M I L K  J E L L Y :** In place of the rose water, use ¼ cupful of orange water (available at Middle Eastern and specialty food stores).

## *Saffron Pudding*

6 TO 8 SERVINGS
PREPARATION: 20 MINUTES
CHILLING TIME: 6 HOURS

Chill a 5-cup serving bowl.

> ½ **cup boiling water**
> ¼ **teaspoon saffron**

Into the water, crumble the saffron; allow it to steep, covered, for 30 minutes. Strain the water and reserve it.

> 2 **envelopes unflavored gelatin**

Over the reserved cooled saffron water, sprinkle the gelatin and allow it to soften for 5 minutes. Dissolve it over simmering water.

> 4 **cups plain yogurt**
> 1 **cup sugar**
> 2 **tablespoons rose** *or* **orange water**
> **Dissolved gelatin-saffron mixture**
> **A pinch of salt**

In the container of an electric blender, combine the yogurt, sugar, rose water, gelatin-saffron water, and salt. Whirl the mixture until the sugar is dissolved. (If more convenient, the ingredients may be combined in a mixing bowl and blended with a rotary beater until the sugar is dissolved.) Transfer the mixture to the serving bowl and chill it for at least 6 hours, or until it is thoroughly set.

> **Crushed toasted almonds** *or* **nutmeg (optional)**

If desired, before serving the dessert, sprinkle it with crushed almonds or fresh-grated nutmeg.

## Sherry Gelatin

6 SERVINGS
PREPARATION: 25 MINUTES
CHILLING TIME: 6 HOURS

Lightly oil and chill a 5-cup ring or other mold.

**2 envelopes unflavored gelatin**
**½ cup cold water**
**1 cup boiling water**

In a mixing bowl, sprinkle the gelatin over the cold water and allow it to soften for 5 minutes. Add the boiling water, stirring to dissolve the gelatin.

**⅔ cup sugar**
**A pinch of salt**

Add the sugar and salt, stirring to dissolve them.

**1½ cups dry sherry**
**1½ cups strained fresh orange juice**
**2 tablespoons strained fresh lemon juice**

Stir in the sherry and the orange and lemon juices. Allow the mixture to cool, transfer it to the prepared mold, and chill it for at least 6 hours, or until it is thoroughly set.

***Crème anglaise*, page 192**

Unmold the gelatin onto a chilled serving plate; offer the sauce separately.

# Creams and Ice Creams

# Creams

In America, the standard "cream" dessert is perhaps Bavarian Cream; the fact that it is airy and light and made with gelatin, like cold mousses and soufflés and, obviously, aspics, is my reason—entirely subjective!—for its inclusion here, together with a few other custards and puddings. The greater part of this section is devoted to Bavarian Cream simply because of the seemingly endless variations of which it is capable. A most versatile dessert!

By definition, creams and custards are more or less pudding-like desserts made of milk and egg and flavorings, simmered or baked, to which gelatin is sometimes added to give body and shape to the finished dish.

Because I enjoy desserts most when they are not too sweet, I egotistically assume that my reader shares my taste; therefore these cream desserts are made with less sugar than, for example, they would be were you to order them in a restaurant. In making them, start with the suggested amount of sugar and, if desired, add more to taste.

Although making creams and custards is easy in its own right, there are a few do's and don't's which, I believe, will facilitate your use of these recipes and which, too, will assure you successful results. For example, never cook creams and custards over high heat; the borderline between to curdle or not to curdle, as the question is considered for desserts, is a matter of a few seconds time or a few degrees Fahrenheit. Stir them *constantly*; they enjoy being pampered. They are best made in the top of a double boiler over simmering—not boiling—water. In the absence of a double boiler, an asbestos mat is good protection against too much heat. If the cream or custard does curdle, pour it into a cold bowl and whip it with a wire whisk or rotary beater, or whirl it for a few seconds in the container of an electric blender.

The term "boiled" custard is a misnomer: A custard which is boiled undergoes metamorphosis with alarming speed to become unacceptable, sweetened scrambled eggs—or something approaching them. As with other creams and custards, simmering under a watchful eye is the best way to success. A little cornstarch (1 teaspoonful for a 4-egg custard) stirred into the milk will help prevent curdling. Also, the less you beat the eggs, the firmer the dessert will be; beating tends to make the cream or custard porous.

If the recipe calls for scalded milk, heat it only until it shimmers and shows the thinnest film on top. If by chance the milk should scorch, discard it and start again; scorched milk gives an "edgy" taste to creams and custards.

*Cooked* custards are done when they leave a light satiny coating on the metal spoon with which you have been stirring them. When they are sufficiently cooked, put the top of the double boiler immediately into cold water; this step will arrest any further cooking.

*Baked* custards, often prepared in individual cups, are cooked by placing the cups (or larger container, if you prefer) in a pan of hot, but not boiling, water. The custard is done when a sharp knife, inserted at the center, comes out clean.

The time required to chill the custard-gelatin mixture "until it just begins to set," or until it is the consistency of heavy syrup, varies for two reasons: the temperature of the liquid itself (was dissolved gelatin stirred into a chilled custard—unlikely in the making of dessert creams —or was the softened gelatin stirred into the hot custard—the customary procedure?) and the temperature of the added ingredient or ingredients (if chilled, the near-jelling time will be considerably reduced). After the custard-gelatin mixture has reached room temperature and the chilled ingredient(s) is added, allow about one hour for the mixture to "just begin to set" or to attain the consistency of heavy syrup.

Finished creams and custards should be refrigerated at once, and for no longer than three or four days. Bacteria like them as much as we do and, for this reason, they are fragile "holders" even under the best of circumstances. Seal them tightly with plastic wrap.

Last, a word about *crème anglaise* or, as we knew it as children, "boiled" or "soft" custard. It is a fine way to use egg yolks remaining from soufflé-making and is a delicious sauce for cold dessert mousses and soufflés as well as a fine smooth dessert in its own right (as Floating Island on page 168, for example). Try it also over halved ripe strawberries, or diced fresh pineapple, or blueberries, or sliced fresh peaches, or . . . enjoy it! It is healthful, easy, and satisfying.

## Almond Cream

6 TO 8 SERVINGS
PREPARATION: 45 MINUTES (NOT INCLUDING CHILLING THE CUSTARD)
CHILLING TIME: 6 HOURS

*An enriched version of Bavarian Cream, page 160.*

Chill a serving dish or 6-cup mold of your choice.

> **1 three-and-one-half-ounce package blanched slivered almonds**

On a baking sheet, spread the almonds evenly; toast them in a 350° oven for 10 to 15 minutes, or until they are a deep golden brown. In the container of a food processor or electric blender, whirl them until they are ground fine. Reserve the almond "flour."

> **1 envelope plus 1 teaspoon unflavored gelatin**
> **1½ cups milk**

In the top of a double boiler, sprinkle the gelatin over the milk and allow it to soften for 5 minutes. Over simmering water, dissolve the gelatin, stirring constantly.

> **2 tablespoons flour**
> **½ cup sugar**
> **A pinch of salt**

Combine the flour, sugar, and salt; add them to the milk and cook the mixture, stirring constantly, for 5 minutes.

> **6 egg yolks, lightly beaten**
> **1 teaspoon almond extract**
> **Reserved almond "flour"**

Away from the heat, whip the egg yolks into the milk mixture. Over simmering water, cook the custard, stirring constantly, until it coats a metal spoon. Stir in the almond extract and almond "flour." Allow the custard to cool and then chill it until it is the consistency of very heavy syrup, just beginning to set.

> 1 **cup heavy cream, whipped**
> 6 **egg whites, beaten until stiff but not dry**

Beat the chilled custard until it is smooth. Fold in the whipped cream. Beat in one-fifth of the egg white; fold in the remainder. Using a rubber spatula, transfer the cream to the serving dish or mold rinsed with cold water. Chill the dessert for at least 6 hours, or until it is thoroughly set. Serve it from the dish or unmold it onto a chilled serving plate.

## Apple Cream

6 SERVINGS
PREPARATION: 25 MINUTES
COOKING: 45 MINUTES IN A 250° OVEN

Butter well a pie tin or other ovenproof dish.

> 3 **medium-size tart apples, peeled, cored, and sliced thin**
>    **lengthwise**
> **Dark rum**

In a mixing bowl, toss the apple slices with rum to coat them well (more rum may be added as necessary). Allow the apple to macerate while you make the cream.

> 2¼ **cups milk**
> 3 **eggs**
> ½ **cup flour**
> ½ **cup sugar**
> 1 **teaspoon vanilla extract**
> **A pinch of salt**

In the container of a food processor or blender, combine the milk, eggs, flour, sugar, vanilla extract, and salt; whirl them until the mixture is thoroughly blended. Transfer it to the prepared dish.

Reserved apple slices
Granulated sugar (optional)

Drain the apples and arrange them radially in an overlapping pattern on top of the cream; if desired, sprinkle them with sugar. Bake the dessert at 250° for 45 minutes, or until it is set. Serve the dessert warm but not hot.

## Avocado Cream

4 SERVINGS
PREPARATION: 15 MINUTES
CHILLING TIME: 3 HOURS

Chill 4 dessert glasses or a serving dish.

> 2 large ripe avocados, peeled, seeded, and chopped coarse
> ¼ cup strained fresh lime juice
> ⅔ cup sugar
> A pinch of salt

In the container of a food processor or electric blender, combine the avocados, lime juice, sugar, and salt; whirl them until they are reduced to a smooth purée. Transfer the mixture to a mixing bowl.

> ½ cup heavy cream, whipped

Into the avocado mixture, fold the whipped cream. Spoon the dessert into the glasses or serving dish and place it in the freezer for at least 3 hours, or until it is set.

## Baked Custard

6 SERVINGS
PREPARATION: 20 MINUTES
COOKING: 20 MINUTES IN A 350° OVEN

Lightly butter 6 individual ovenproof custard cups.

> 2 cups milk

Scald the milk and allow it to cool slightly.

> 2 eggs
> 2 egg yolks
> 3 tablespoons sugar
> A pinch of salt
> ½ teaspoon vanilla extract

In a mixing bowl, combine the eggs, egg yolks, sugar, salt, and vanilla extract. Using a fork, blend the mixture well (do not use a beater). Add a little of the scalded milk, stirring; then add the egg mixture to the remaining milk, stirring to blend the mixture well. Pour the mixture into the prepared cups; put them in a pan of hot water. Bake the custards at 350° for 20 minutes, or until a sharp knife inserted in the center comes out clean.

## Basic Recipe for Bavarian Cream

6 TO 8 SERVINGS (THE RECIPE MAY BE DOUBLED AND REFRIGERATED)
PREPARATION: 25 MINUTES (DOES NOT INCLUDE CHILLING THE CUSTARD)
CHILLING TIME: 6 HOURS

*Similar to a cold soufflé in that both are made with gelatin, separated eggs, and cream, this dessert is easily molded and can be turned out onto a chilled serving platter to make a rather handsome presentation. Capable of many flavor variations, Bavarian Cream is always a smooth and festive ending to a meal.*

Chill a serving dish or 6-cup mold of your choice.

> 1 envelope unflavored gelatin
> ½ cup sugar
> A pinch of salt

In the top of a double boiler, blend the gelatin, sugar, and salt.

> 1½ cups milk
> 3 egg yolks

Combine the milk and egg yolks and, using a rotary beater, blend the mixture well; add it to the contents of the double boiler. Over simmering water, cook the custard, stirring constantly, until it coats a metal spoon. Remove it from the heat.

1½ teaspoons vanilla

Stir in the vanilla. Allow the mixture to cool and then chill it until it is the consistency of very heavy syrup, just beginning to set.

1 cup heavy cream, whipped
3 egg whites, beaten until stiff but not dry

Beat the chilled custard until it is smooth. Fold in the whipped cream. Beat in one-fifth of the egg white; fold in the remainder. Using a rubber spatula, transfer the cream to the serving dish or mold rinsed with cold water. Chill the dessert for at least 6 hours, or until it is thoroughly set. Serve it from the dish or unmold it onto a chilled serving plate.

APPLE BAVARIAN CREAM: Use 1 envelope plus 1 teaspoonful of unflavored gelatin. Use 1¼ cups milk. To the hot custard, add 3 tart apples, peeled and grated fine, the grated rind and strained juice of 1 small lemon, and the vanilla, as called for. Complete the basic recipe as written.

BANANA BAVARIAN CREAM: To the hot custard, add 1 large very ripe banana or 2 small ones, puréed (the fullness of flavor depends upon the ripeness of the fruit). Complete the basic recipe as written.

CHOCOLATE BAVARIAN CREAM: In the milk, before adding the gelatin-sugar mixture, melt 1 six-ounce package of semisweet chocolate bits; make sure that the chocolate is completely melted and the mixture smooth. Add the gelatin-sugar mixture and complete the basic recipe as written.

COCONUT BAVARIAN CREAM: In place of the milk as called for, use 1 fifteen-ounce can "cream of coconut" (available at specialty food stores and many supermarkets), plus milk to equal 1½ cups. Omit the sugar. Complete the basic recipe as written. Before chilling, sprinkle the custard with toasted shredded coconut.

CHERRY BAVARIAN CREAM: Use the liquid from 1 one-pound can of water-pack pitted sour cherries plus milk to equal 1½ cups. To the hot custard, add the cherries, coarsely chopped; in place of the vanilla, use ¼ teaspoonful of almond extract. Complete the basic recipe as written.

COFFEE BAVARIAN CREAM: To the hot custard, add 2 tablespoonfuls of instant coffee powder. Complete the basic recipe as written.

CRANBERRY BAVARIAN CREAM: Cook fresh cranberries as directed on the package; reserve 1½ cups and add them to the hot custard. Omit the sugar; in place of the vanilla, use a drop or two of almond extract. Complete the basic recipe as written.

DANISH CREAM: Make the custard with 2 cupfuls of scalded light cream and into it stir ½ cupful of crushed toasted almonds.

FRUIT-BASED BAVARIAN CREAM: Use 1 envelope plus 1 teaspoonful of unflavored gelatin. To the hot custard, add 1 cupful of purée of your choice:

BERRY (black–, blue–, rasp–, or strawberry): In place of the vanilla, use ¼ teaspoonful almond extract.

GUAVA (available canned): Use the reserved liquid plus milk to equal 1½ cups.

KUMQUAT, page 197.

MANGO (available canned): Use the reserved liquid plus milk to equal 1½ cups.

PAPAYA (available canned): Use the reserved liquid plus milk to equal 1½ cups.

PEACH: Use very ripe fresh fruit to make the purée.

PEAR: Use very ripe fresh fruit to make the purée, or you may use 1 twenty-ounce can of pears.

PERSIMMON: After the addition of the purée, use more sugar, if needed, to taste.

PINEAPPLE: Use 1 eight-ounce can of crushed pineapple with its liquid.

PRUNE: Use 1 one-pound jar of pitted, puréed prunes. Use the reserved liquid plus milk to equal 1½ cups.

QUINCE (available canned): Use the liquid plus milk to equal 1½ cups.

GINGER BAVARIAN CREAM: Mix ¾ teaspoonful of powdered ginger with the gelatin, sugar, and salt. After the addition of the whipped cream and egg white, gently fold in ½ cupful of candied ginger, chopped fine. Complete the basic recipe as written.

HAZELNUT BAVARIAN CREAM: After the addition of the whipped cream and egg white, gently fold in 1½ cupfuls of crushed hazelnuts. Complete the basic recipe as written.

LEMON BAVARIAN CREAM: To the hot custard, add the grated rind and strained juice of 2 medium-size lemons; omit the vanilla; adjust the quantity of sugar to taste. Complete the basic recipe as written.

LIME BAVARIAN CREAM: To the hot custard, add the grated rind of 1 large lime and the strained juice of 2 limes; omit the vanilla; adjust the quantity of sugar to taste. Add a few drops of green food coloring, if desired. Complete the basic recipe as written.

MINT BAVARIAN CREAM: To the hot custard, add ¼ cupful of fine-chopped fresh mint leaves; in place of the vanilla, use ½ teaspoonful of mint extract. Complete the basic recipe as written.

ORANGE BAVARIAN CREAM: To the hot custard, add the grated rind and strained juice of 1 large orange; in place of the vanilla, use 1 teaspoonful of orange extract. Complete the basic recipe as written.

PEANUT-BRITTLE BAVARIAN CREAM: After the addition of the whipped cream and egg white, fold in ½ to ¾ cupful of peanut brittle, crushed. Complete the basic recipe as written.

PEPPERMINT-STICK BAVARIAN CREAM: Follow the directions for Peanut-Brittle Bavarian Cream, using ½ cupful of crushed peppermint candy. Complete the basic recipe as written.

PISTACHIO BAVARIAN CREAM: To the hot custard, add ½ cupful of crushed pistachio nuts and a few drops of green food coloring. Complete the basic recipe as written.

**POMEGRANATE-FLAVORED BAVARIAN CREAM:** Reduce the milk to ½ cupful and add 1 cupful of grenadine syrup; omit the sugar. Complete the basic recipe as written.

**ROSE-FLAVORED BAVARIAN CREAM:** To the cooled custard, add ¼ cupful of rose water (available at Middle Eastern and specialty food stores); omit the vanilla. Complete the basic recipe as written. (If desired, you may prepare the recipe using the same quantity of orange-blossom water. These Bavarian Creams are very delicately flavored.)

**RUM BAVARIAN CREAM:** To the hot custard, add ½ cupful of dark rum; omit the vanilla. Complete the basic recipe as written.

**CHARLOTTE RUSSE** (8 to 10 servings): An elegant classic dessert based on Bavarian Cream.

Line a 9-inch spring-form pan with split ladyfingers (about 20); sprinkle them with ¼ cupful of light rum, cream sherry, Marsala, or orange-flavored liqueur. (Rum is the flavor generally used, but the others are very good, too.) Double the basic recipe for Bavarian Cream, omitting the egg whites. Complete the recipe as written. Unmold the Charlotte onto a chilled serving plate and offer it cut in wedges, as you would serve a cake.

**SPANISH CREAM** (a richer Bavarian Cream): Increase the milk to 2 cupfuls; increase the egg yolks to 4; increase the egg whites to 4. Complete the basic recipe as written. Serve the dessert with sliced or crushed fresh fruit.

## *Basic Recipe for Blancmange*

6 SERVINGS
PREPARATION: 20 MINUTES
CHILLING TIME: 3 HOURS

> 6 tablespoons cornstarch
> ⅔ cup sugar
> ¼ teaspoon salt

In the top of a double boiler, sift together the cornstarch, sugar, and salt.

4 cups milk

Gradually add the milk, stirring until the mixture is smooth. Over simmering water, cook, stirring, until it is thickened. Remove it from the heat.

2 teaspoons vanilla extract

Stir in the vanilla. Transfer the dessert to a 5-cup mold or serving dish, allow it to cool, and chill it for 3 hours.

**Crushed fresh fruit of your choice ( optional )**

If desired, unmold the *blancmange* onto a chilled serving plate and garnish it with the fruit.

CHOCOLATE BLANCMANGE: Increase the cornstarch to 7 tablespoonfuls, increase the sugar to 1⅓ cupfuls; into the cornstarch-sugar-salt mixture, stir 3 squares of bitter chocolate (3 ounces), grated. Reduce the vanilla extract to 1 teaspoonful.

COCONUT BLANCMANGE: Omit the sugar; mix the cornstarch and salt in ½ cupful of milk. As the principal liquid ingredient, use 1 fifteen-ounce can of coconut cream, plus milk, to equal 3½ cupfuls. Garnish the dessert with toasted shredded coconut.

FRUIT BLANCMANGE: Prepare the basic recipe as written, using as the liquid ingredient 2 cupfuls of milk and 2 cupfuls of puréed fruit of your choice.

LEMON BLANCMANGE: Increase the cornstarch to 7 tablespoonfuls, increase the sugar to 1 cupful; use 3½ cupfuls of milk and when the mixture is thickened, stir in ½ cupful of strained fresh lemon juice and the grated rind of 1 medium-size lemon. In place of the vanilla extract, use 1 teaspoonful of lemon extract.

ORANGE BLANCMANGE: Increase the cornstarch to 7 tablespoonfuls; as the liquid ingredient, use 2 cupfuls each of milk and strained fresh orange juice. In place of the vanilla extract, use 1 teaspoonful of orange extract and the grated rind of 1 medium-size orange.

## Buttermilk Cream

6 SERVINGS
PREPARATION: 30 MINUTES
CHILLING TIME: 6 HOURS

>  2 envelopes unflavored gelatin, softened for 5 minutes in
>    ½ cup cold water

Over simmering water, dissolve the gelatin and reserve it.

>  1 cup strained fresh orange juice
>  1½ cups sugar
>  A pinch of salt

In a mixing bowl, combine the orange juice, sugar, and salt. Stir the
mixture until the sugar is dissolved.

>  2½ cups buttermilk
>  Reserved gelatin

Stir in the buttermilk and gelatin. Transfer the cream to a chilled
serving dish and chill it for at least 6 hours, or until it is thoroughly set.

>  Whipped cream (optional)

Garnish each serving with a dollop of whipped cream.


## Coeur à la Crème

6 SERVINGS
PREPARATION: 25 MINUTES
CHILLING TIME: 6 HOURS

Lightly oil and chill a 5-cup (traditionally heart-shaped) mold.

>  1 envelope gelatin, softened for 5 minutes in ¼ cup cold
>    water

Over simmering water, dissolve the gelatin and reserve it.

>  1 pound cream-style cottage cheese, at room temperature
>  2 three-ounce packages cream cheese, at room temperature

In the container of a food processor or blender, whirl the two cheeses until the mixture is smooth.

> **Reserved gelatin**
> **3 tablespoons sugar**
> **A pinch of salt**
> **1½ teaspoons vanilla extract**

To the contents of the container, add the gelatin, sugar, salt, and vanilla extract. Whirl the mixture to dissolve the sugar. Transfer it to a mixing bowl.

> **¾ cup heavy cream**
> **4 tablespoons sugar**

In a mixing bowl, whip the cream, gradually adding the sugar by the single tablespoonful. Into the cheese mixture, fold the whipped cream. Transfer the dessert to the prepared mold and chill it for at least 6 hours, or until it is thoroughly set.

> **Large ripe strawberries, rinsed but unhulled**

Onto a chilled serving plate, unmold the *coeur à la crème* and garnish the plate with the strawberries, to be eaten out of hand.

## Crème Brûlée

6 SERVINGS
PREPARATION: 30 MINUTES (THE PREPARATION TIME DOES NOT INCLUDE
    THE INITIAL CHILLING)
CHILLING TIME: 4 HOURS

*Despite its French name, Burnt Cream may well be an English dessert; also known as Cambridge Cream, it was first enjoyed, according to tradition, at that celebrated university in a time as remote as that of Good Queen Bess.*

> **2 cups heavy cream**

In the top of a double boiler, scald the cream.

> **8 egg yolks (4 whole eggs will substitute)**
> **¼ cup sugar**
> **A pinch of salt**

In a mixing bowl, beat together until smooth the egg yolks, sugar, and salt. Gradually add the scalded cream, stirring constantly. Return the mixture to the double boiler and, over simmering water, cook it, stirring constantly, until it coats the spoon. Strain the custard into an ovenproof serving dish in a layer no deeper than 1½ inches. Allow it to cool and then chill it for the prescribed length of time.

**¼ cup granulated or dark brown sugar**

Over the top of the chilled custard, sift the sugar. Place the dish under the broiler for a few minutes, or until the sugar is melted. Remove the dessert at once and chill it for 4 hours, or until the glaze is brittle.

*Variation:*

   **BURNT PUMPKIN CREAM**: To the hot custard, add 1½ cupfuls of pumpkin purée seasoned with ¼ teaspoonful of ground allspice, ¾ teaspoonful of cinnamon, and ½ teaspoonful of ground ginger; increase the salt to ¼ teaspoonful.

## Floating Island

4 SERVINGS

PREPARATION: 40 MINUTES (THE PREPARATION TIME DOES NOT INCLUDE CHILLING THE CUSTARD)

Prepare *Crème anglaise*, page 192; transfer it to an ovenproof serving dish and chill it.

   **Egg whites remaining from *Crème anglaise* recipe**
   **A pinch of salt**
   **¼ cup sugar**

In a mixing bowl, combine the egg whites and salt; beat them, gradually adding the sugar, until they stand in stiff peaks. With the meringue, make four "islands" on top of the chilled custard. Put the dish on the top shelf of a preheated 500° oven for 3 minutes, or until the meringue is tinged with brown.

## Honey Cream

6 SERVINGS
PREPARATION: 20 MINUTES
COOKING: 30 MINUTES IN A 375° OVEN

 2 cups light cream
 ¼ cup honey
 A pinch of salt

In a saucepan, scald the cream. Add the honey and salt, stirring until the mixture is homogenous.

 3 eggs, lightly beaten

Into the eggs, pour some of the hot cream, stirring; then pour the egg mixture into the remaining cream, stirring to blend it well. Transfer the mixture to individual ovenproof cups; place them in a pan of hot water, and bake the honey creams at 375° for 30 minutes, or until a sharp knife inserted in the center comes out clean.

 A grating of nutmeg

Garnish the creams with nutmeg, allow them to cool, and then chill them.

## Lime Cream

6 SERVINGS
PREPARATION: 30 MINUTES
CHILLING TIME: 2 HOURS

Chill a 4-cup serving bowl.

 1 cup sugar
 2 tablespoons cornstarch
 A pinch of salt

In a saucepan, sift together the sugar, cornstarch, and salt.

 ¼ cup strained fresh lime juice
 Grated rind of 1 lime

Add the lime juice and rind, stirring until the mixture is smooth.

**1 egg, lightly beaten**

Add the egg and, over gentle heat, cook the mixture, stirring, for 2 minutes. Allow it to cool.

**1 teaspoon vanilla extract**
**1 cup heavy cream, whipped**

Stir in the vanilla extract and fold in the whipped cream. Transfer the dessert to the serving bowl; chill for 2 hours.

**Grated rind of 1 lime**

When serving the lime cream, garnish it with the grated rind.


## Orange Cream

6 SERVINGS
PREPARATION: 30 MINUTES
CHILLING TIME: 4 HOURS

Chill a 4-cup serving dish or 6 individual dessert glasses.

**4 tablespoons cornstarch**
**½ cup sugar**
**¼ teaspoon salt**

In the top of a double boiler, sift together the cornstarch, sugar, and salt.

**1 cup unsweetened evaporated milk**
**1 cup strained fresh orange juice**

Add the liquids, stirring until the mixture is smooth.

**1 egg, lightly beaten**
**1 tablespoon strained fresh lemon juice**
**Grated rind of 1 medium-size orange**

Stir in the egg, lemon juice, and orange rind. Over simmering water, cook the mixture, stirring, until it thickens. Transfer it to a chilled serving dish or individual dessert glasses. Allow the cream to cool and then chill it.

## Port Wine Cream

6 SERVINGS
PREPARATION: 30 MINUTES
CHILLING TIME: 3 HOURS

Chill a 5-cup serving bowl.

> 6 tablespoons butter, at room temperature
> 2 cups confectioners sugar, sifted
> A pinch of salt

In a mixing bowl, combine the butter, sugar, and salt. Beat the mixture until it is light and fluffy.

> ⅓ cup port wine
> 2 tablespoons Cognac (optional)
> Strained juice of 1 medium-size lemon

Combine the port wine, Cognac, and lemon juice and beat the mixture into the contents of the mixing bowl.

> 1 cup heavy cream, whipped
> 2 egg whites, beaten until stiff but not dry

Fold in the whipped cream. Beat in one-fifth of the egg white; fold in the remainder. Using a rubber spatula, transfer the cream to the serving bowl and chill it for at least 3 hours.

## Pots de Crème

6 SERVINGS
PREPARATION: 25 MINUTES
CHILLING TIME: 4 HOURS

Chill 6 individual custard cups or *pots de crème.*

> 2 cups heavy cream
> 1 square (1 ounce) unsweetened chocolate, grated
> 6 tablespoons sugar
> A pinch of salt

In the top of a double boiler, combine the cream, chocolate, sugar, and salt. Over simmering water, cook the mixture, stirring, until the chocolate is melted and the sugar dissolved.

**4 egg yolks, beaten**

Add the egg yolks and cook the mixture, stirring constantly, until it is thickened and coats the spoon.

**¼ teaspoon vanilla extract**

Stir in the vanilla extract. Transfer the dessert to the chilled cups, allow it to cool, and refrigerate it for 4 hours.

*Variations:*

COFFEE POTS DE CRÈME : In place of the chocolate, use 2 generous tablespoonfuls of instant coffee powder.

POTS DE CRÈME IN THE BLENDER (not the real thing, but a very acceptable substitute): In the container of an electric blender, combine 1 six-ounce package of semisweet chocolate bits, 2 eggs, and 1 teaspoonful of vanilla extract. In a saucepan, combine ¾ cupful of milk, 2 tablespoonfuls of sugar, and a pinch of salt. Bring the milk to the boil, stirring constantly to dissolve the sugar. Turn on the blender motor and immediately, in a steady stream, pour in the boiling milk. Blend the dessert until the chocolate is melted and the mixture smooth and homogenous. Pour into 6 individual chilled cups and refrigerate it for at least 4 hours.

## Pumpkin Custard

6 SERVINGS
PREPARATION: 25 MINUTES
COOKING: 50 MINUTES IN A 325° OVEN
CHILLING TIME: 4 HOURS

Lightly oil a 5 cup mold.

2 cups pumpkin purée
4 eggs
½ cup sugar
1 fourteen-ounce can
   evaporated milk, plus
   water to equal 2 cups

1 tablespoon flour
1 teaspoon grated
   orange rind
½ teaspoon ground
   allspice
A pinch of salt

In a mixing bowl, combine the pumpkin purée, eggs, sugar, milk, flour, orange rind, allspice, and salt. Using a rotary beater blend the mixture until it is smooth.

Transfer the mixture to the prepared mold, place the mold in a pan of hot water, and bake the custard at 325° for 50 minutes, or until a sharp knife inserted in the center comes out clean. Allow the custard to cool and then chill it.

*Crème anglaise*, page 192

Unmold the custard onto a chilled serving plate; offer the sauce separately.

## Rose-water Cream

4 SERVINGS
PREPARATION: 25 MINUTES
CHILLING TIME: 6 HOURS

*The recipe may also be made with orange water.*

Chill a 4-cup serving bowl.

1 envelope unflavored gelatin, softened for 5 minutes in
   ¼ cup cold water

Soften the gelatin and reserve it.

1 cup light cream
⅔ cup sugar
A pinch of salt

In the top of a double boiler, combine the cream, sugar, and salt. Over simmering water, heat the mixture, stirring to dissolve the sugar. Add the reserved gelatin, stirring to dissolve it. Allow the mixture to cool. Transfer it to a mixing bowl.

**3 tablespoons rose water**
**1 cup sour cream**

Add the rose water and sour cream, stirring until the mixture is smooth and homogenous. Chill it until it just begins to set. With a rotary beater, whip the dessert until it is fluffy. Transfer it to the prepared bowl and chill for at least 6 hours.

**Sliced or crushed fruit of your choice (optional)**

Serve the rose-water cream garnished, if you like, with sliced or crushed fruit.


## Zabaglione

4 TO 6 SERVINGS
PREPARATION: 15 MINUTES
CHILLING TIME: 1 HOUR

Chill 4 to 6 individual serving glasses.

**6 egg yolks**
**6 tablespoons sugar**
**6 tablespoons Marsala wine**
**A pinch of salt**

In the top of a double boiler, combine the egg yolks, sugar, Marsala, and salt. Beat the mixture until it is smooth and light. Over simmering water, cook it, stirring, until the sugar is dissolved and it is thickened. Transfer it to a mixing bowl. Allow it to cool.

**½ cup heavy cream, whipped**

Fold in the whipped cream. Transfer the dessert to the prepared glasses and chill it for at least 1 hour.

*Variations:*

Marsala wine is the traditional flavoring agent of this celebrated Italian cream, but you may also use, if desired, dry white wine, dry sherry, or dry vermouth.

## Zuppa Inglese

4 TO 6 SERVINGS
PREPARATION: 25 MINUTES
CHILLING TIME: 3 HOURS

Chill a 3½-cup serving bowl.

**2 cups milk**
**2 tablespoons butter**

In the top of a double boiler, combine the milk and butter. Scald the milk.

**½ cup sugar**
**3 tablespoons cornstarch**
**¼ teaspoon salt**

Sift together the sugar, cornstarch, and salt; add them to the scalded milk and, over simmering water, cook the mixture, stirring, until it is thickened.

**2 eggs, beaten**

Add the eggs and continue cooking the custard for 2 minutes.

**Marsala wine, to taste, *or* 1 teaspoon vanilla extract**

Stir in the wine or vanilla extract. Transfer the cream to a serving bowl and cover it with plastic wrap resting on its surface (to prevent its crusting); chill it.

**Sponge cake *or* cut fresh fruits of your choice**

Serve the *zuppa inglese* over sponge cake or with fruit.

# Ice Creams

The ice-cream recipes offered here are perhaps unusual, deriving as they do from ideas which originally came to me at random. There are many and excellent sources for standard ice-cream flavors; for this reason, I have selected recipes you may not find elsewhere. As always, my hope is that you will be led to explore the possibilities for unusual ice creams; they are fun to make (a fine party can be made of turning the freezer crank), capable of almost limitless originality, and delicious to eat.

## Basic Recipe for Ice Cream

YIELD: ABOUT 1½ QUARTS
PREPARATION: 30 MINUTES

The freezing time will depend upon the method used, page 177.

> 1½ cups light cream
> ½ cup sugar
> ¼ teaspoon salt

In the top of a double boiler, scald the cream. Add the sugar and salt, stirring until they are dissolved. Remove the mixture from the heat.

> 4 egg yolks, lightly beaten
> Special ingredient(s), as called for

176

To the egg yolks, add a little of the hot cream, stirring constantly. In a steady stream, stir the egg mixture into the remaining cream. Over simmering water, cook the custard, stirring constantly, until it coats the spoon. Remove it from the heat, stir in the solid ingredient(s), as required, allow it to cool, and chill it.

Special seasonings, as called for ( vanilla extract, almond
   extract, etc. )
2 cups chilled heavy cream, two days old

Into the chilled custard, stir the seasonings, as required, and the heavy cream. Freeze the ice cream in your preferred way.

CALORIE-COUNTER ICE CREAM (less rich, more economical, and not quite as seductively delicious as the recipe above): In place of the light cream, use an equal quantity of milk; sift the sugar and salt with 1 tablespoonful of cornstarch before adding the mixture to the milk; in place of the heavy cream, use 2 cupfuls of light cream, two days old.

## To Freeze Ice Cream

*In an Ice-Cream Freezer:* Pour the prepared mixture into the can of the ice-cream freezer; adjust the dasher; cover the can with its lid; place the can in the freezer bucket; put on the gear case so that the handle turns easily. Pack the bucket with one part rock salt to eight parts crushed ice. Churn the custard in a steady rhythm until it is very difficult to turn the freezer handle (at this point the mixture will have achieved its maximum density). During the churning, add salt and ice as necessary in the proportions given. Remove the gear case, lid, and dasher; with a rubber spatula, clean the dasher, adding the drippings to the contents of the freezer can. Cover the can with aluminum foil and replace the lid. Allow the ice cream to stand for 2 hours, either in the freezer bucket or in the freezer compartment of the refrigerator.

*In Freezer Trays:* Pour the prepared mixture into deep freezer trays or other utensil and freeze it until it is solid for ½ inch around the edge. Transfer it to a mixing bowl and beat it vigorously until it is smooth. (If you use this freezing method, at this point, add the prepared solid ingredient.) Return the mixture to the freezing compartment until it is firm.

*In an In-the-Freezer Freezer:* There is available at modest cost an appliance which works electrically on the principle of the dasher-freezer and which one puts in the freezing compartment of the refrigerator. It is reliable for smooth ice creams but less effective for those with solid ingredients.

**ALMOND ICE CREAM:** To the hot custard, add ½ to ¾ cupful of crushed toasted almonds; into the chilled custard, before adding the heavy cream, stir 1½ teaspoonfuls of almond extract. Complete the basic recipe as written.

**APRICOT ICE CREAM:** In a saucepan, combine ¾ of a pound of tenderized dried apricots, ½ a lime, sliced thin and seeded, and 1 cupful of water; simmer the apricots, uncovered, for 30 minutes, or until they are very tender. Discard the lime slices; in the container of a food processor or blender, purée the apricots with their cooking liquid and reserve them. Make the custard with 1 cupful of light cream and ¾ cupful of sugar; to the hot custard, add the apricot purée. Into the chilled custard, before adding the heavy cream, stir ¼ teaspoonful of almond extract. Complete the basic recipe as written.

**AVOCADO ICE CREAM:** Make the custard with 1 cupful of light cream and ¾ cupful of sugar; to the hot custard, add 1 large ripe avocado, peeled, seeded, chopped coarse, and puréed, with the contents of 1 six-ounce container of frozen orange juice concentrate and 3 tablespoonfuls of strained fresh lemon juice. Complete the basic recipe as written.

**BANANA ICE CREAM:** To the hot custard, add 3 large, very ripe bananas, puréed with the strained juice of ½ lemon; into the chilled custard, before adding the heavy cream, stir a drop or two of almond extract. Complete the basic recipe as written.

**BLACKBERRY OR BLUEBERRY ICE CREAM:** Stem, pick over, rinse, and drain 1 quart of blackberries or blueberries; stew them with ½ cupful of sugar, or more to taste, until they are very very soft; strain them, reserving the purée. Make the custard with 1 cupful of light cream and omit the sugar; to the hot custard, add the berry purée. Into the chilled custard, before adding the heavy cream, stir a drop or two of almond extract. Complete the basic recipe as written.

CHESTNUT ICE CREAM: Omit the sugar when making the custard; into the hot custard, stir the contents of 1 fifteen-ounce can of sweetened chestnut purée. Into the chilled custard, before adding the heavy cream, stir 1½ teaspoonfuls of vanilla extract. Complete the basic recipe as written.

CRANBERRY ICE CREAM: In a saucepan, combine 1 one-pound package of cranberries, 1 six-ounce container of frozen orange-juice concentrate, thawed, 1 cupful of sugar and a pinch of salt. Over high heat, cook the cranberries, stirring, until they burst; reduce the heat and simmer them, uncovered, for 20 minutes. Make the custard with 1 cupful of light cream; omit the sugar. To the hot custard, add the prepared cranberries. Complete the basic recipe as written.

DAMSON PLUM ICE CREAM: Omit the sugar when making the custard; into the hot custard, stir 1 twelve-ounce jar of damson plum preserves. Into the chilled custard, before adding the heavy cream, stir a drop or two of almond extract. Complete the basic recipe as written.

DATE ICE CREAM: In a saucepan, combine 1 eight-ounce package of pitted dates, chopped fine, and 1 cupful of light cream; simmer the dates, covered, for 10 minutes, or until they are tender. Make the custard with 1 cupful of light cream; to the hot custard, add the dates and their liquid. Into the chilled custard, before adding the heavy cream, stir 1 teaspoonful of vanilla extract. Complete the basic recipe as written.

FIG ICE CREAM: In a saucepan, combine 8 ounces of dried figs, chopped fine, and 1 cupful of light cream; simmer the figs, covered, for 25 minutes, or until they are tender. Make the custard with 1 cupful of light cream; to the hot custard, add the figs and their liquid. Into the chilled custard, before adding the heavy cream, stir 1 teaspoonful of vanilla extract. Complete the basic recipe as written.

GINGER ICE CREAM: In a saucepan, combine ½ pound ginger root, peeled and cut into fine dice, ½ cupful of sugar, 1 cupful of water, and a pinch of salt. Simmer the ginger, uncovered, for 30 minutes, or until it is very tender and the liquid is syrupy; cool and then chill the mixture. When making the custard, use 1 cupful of light cream and ¼ cupful of sugar sifted with 1 teaspoonful of ground ginger; to the hot custard, add the prepared ginger and its syrup. Into the chilled custard, before adding the heavy cream, stir 1 teaspoonful of vanilla extract. Complete the basic recipe as written.

ICE CREAM AU GRAND MARNIER: Use 1 cupful of light cream to make the custard; into the hot custard, stir ⅓ cupful of Grand Marnier or other orange-flavored liqueur. Into the chilled custard, before adding the heavy cream, stir 1½ teaspoonfuls of orange extract. Complete the basic recipe as written.

GUAVA ICE CREAM: Make the custard with 1 cupful of light cream; to the hot custard, add the purée made from the drained contents of 2 fifteen-ounce cans of guava shells and the strained juice of 1 medium-size lemon. Into the chilled custard, before adding the heavy cream, stir a drop or two of almond extract. Complete the basic recipe as written.

HONEY-FLAVORED ICE CREAM: In place of the sugar, use 1 cupful of strong-flavored honey (such as buckwheat, for example); into the chilled custard, before adding the heavy cream, stir 1 teaspoonful of vanilla extract. Complete the basic recipe as written.

KUMQUAT ICE CREAM: To the hot custard, add 2 cupfuls of Kumquats Prepared for Cooking, page 197. Into the chilled custard, before adding the heavy cream, stir ¼ teaspoonful of almond extract. Complete the basic recipe as written.

LEMON ICE CREAM: Make the custard with 1 cupful of light cream and 1½ cupfuls of sugar; to the hot custard, add the grated rind of 2 medium-size lemons. Into the chilled custard, before adding the heavy cream, stir ½ cupful of strained fresh lemon juice and 1 teaspoonful of lemon extract. Complete the basic recipe as written.

MANGO ICE CREAM: Make the custard with 1 cupful of light cream; to the hot custard, add the purée made from the drained contents of 2 fifteen-ounce cans of sliced mango. Into the chilled custard, before adding the heavy cream, stir a drop or two of almond extract. Complete the basic recipe as written.

MAPLE ICE CREAM: Omit the sugar; use in its place 1 cupful of real maple syrup, boiled gently, uncovered, for 10 minutes. Into the chilled custard, before adding the heavy cream, stir 1 teaspoonful of maple flavoring. Complete the basic recipe as written.

MINCEMEAT ICE CREAM: In a saucepan, crumble the contents of 1 nine-ounce package of dehydrated mincemeat and add 1 cupful of water; bring the liquid to the boil and cook the mincemeat, covered, for 5 minutes; reduce the heat and simmer the mixture, uncovered, for 20 minutes, or until it thickens. Into the mincemeat, stir the juice and grated rind of 1 medium-size lemon. To the hot custard, add the prepared mincemeat; into the chilled custard, before adding the heavy cream, stir 1 teaspoonful of vanilla extract. Complete the basic recipe as written.

MINT ICE CREAM: Increase the sugar to 1 cupful; to the hot custard, add 2 cupfuls, lightly packed, of fine-chopped fresh mint leaves. Into the chilled custard, before adding the heavy cream, stir 1 teaspoonful of peppermint extract. Complete the basic recipe as written.

NESSELRODE ICE CREAM: In a mixing bowl, combine ¾ pound of mixed candied fruit and ½ cupful of dark rum; allow the fruit to macerate, stirring it occasionally, for 24 hours (more rum may be added as needed). Make the custard with 1 cupful of light cream; to the hot custard, add the candied fruits and their liquid. Into the chilled custard, before adding the heavy cream, stir 1 teaspoonful of vanilla extract. Complete the basic recipe as written.

PAPAYA ICE CREAM: Make the custard with 1 cupful of light cream; to the hot custard, add the purée made from the drained contents of 2 fifteen-ounce cans of sliced papaya. Into the chilled custard, before adding the heavy cream, stir a drop or two of almond extract. Complete the basic recipe as written.

PEACH ICE CREAM: Make the custard with 1 cupful of light cream; to the hot custard, add the purée made from 6 large ripe peaches, peeled and seeded. Into the chilled custard, before adding the heavy cream, stir a drop or two of almond extract. Complete the basic recipe as written.

*Variation:*

If desired, ¼ cupful of fine-chopped crystallized ginger may be added to the hot custard, together with the peach purée.

PEANUT-BRITTLE ICE CREAM: Into the chilled custard, before adding the heavy cream, stir 1 teaspoonful of vanilla extract. Complete the basic recipe as written and start to freeze the ice cream. When the freezer crank offers resistance, or when the contents of the freezer trays become mushy, add 1½ cupfuls of crushed peanut brittle. Continue to freeze the ice cream until it is set.

PEAR ICE CREAM: Make the custard with 1 cupful of light cream; to the hot custard, add the purée made from 5 large, very ripe pears, peeled and cored. Into the chilled custard, before adding the heavy cream, stir ¼ cupful of pear liqueur. Complete the basic recipe as written.

PERSIMMON ICE CREAM: Make the custard with 1 cupful of light cream and ¾ cupful of sugar; to the hot custard, add 1½ cupfuls of strained persimmon pulp and the strained juice of 1 small lemon. Into the chilled custard, before adding the heavy cream, stir 1 teaspoonful of vanilla extract. Complete the basic recipe as written.

PINEAPPLE ICE CREAM: Make the custard with 1 cupful of light cream and ¾ cupful of sugar; to the hot custard, add the coarse-grated, drained pulp of 1 medium, very ripe pineapple. Into the chilled custard, before adding the heavy cream, stir 1 teaspoonful of vanilla extract. Complete the basic recipe as written.

PRUNE ICE CREAM: Soak overnight in 1 cupful of Cognac the contents of 1 eleven-ounce package of tenderized pitted prunes, chopped coarse; drain and purée the prunes in the container of a food processor or blender. Make the custard with 1 cupful of light cream; to the hot custard, add the prune purée. Into the chilled custard, before adding the heavy cream, stir 1 teaspoonful of vanilla extract. Complete the basic recipe as written.

**PUMPKIN ICE CREAM :** Make the custard with 1 cupful of light cream; to the hot custard, add 1½ cups pumpkin purée seasoned with ½ teaspoonful each of ground allspice, ginger, and nutmeg, 1 teaspoonful of cinnamon, and the strained juice of 1 medium-size lemon. Into the chilled custard, before adding the heavy cream, stir 1 teaspoonful of vanilla extract. Complete the basic recipe as written.

**RAISIN ICE CREAM :** Soak overnight in 1 cupful of dark rum the contents of 1 eleven-ounce package of raisins. Make the custard with 1 cupful of light cream; to the hot custard, add the raisins and their liquid. Into the chilled custard, before adding the heavy cream, stir 1 teaspoonful of vanilla extract. Complete the basic recipe as written.

**RASPBERRY ICE CREAM :** Make the custard with 1 cupful of light cream; to the hot custard, add the strained contents of 2 ten-ounce packages of frozen raspberries. Into the chilled custard, before adding the heavy cream, stir ½ teaspoonful of lemon extract. Complete the basic recipe as written.

**RHUBARB ICE CREAM :** Stew 3 cupfuls of diced rhubarb with ¾ cupful of sugar; add the juice of 1 small lemon and a few drops of red food coloring. Make the custard with 1 cupful of light cream; to the hot custard, add the prepared rhubarb. Into the chilled custard, before adding the heavy cream, stir 1 teaspoonful of vanilla extract. Complete the basic recipe as written.

**STRAWBERRY ICE CREAM :** Make the custard with 1 cupful of light cream and ¾ cupful of sugar; to the hot custard, add 1 quart of ripe strawberries, hulled, rinsed, drained, and puréed. Into the chilled custard, before adding the heavy cream, stir ½ teaspoonful of vanilla extract. Complete the basic recipe as written.

**TEABERRY- or WINTERGREEN-STICK ICE CREAM :** Into the chilled custard, before adding the heavy cream, stir 1 teaspoonful of vanilla extract. Complete the basic recipe as written and start to freeze the ice cream. When the freezer crank offers resistance or when the contents of the freezer trays become mushy, add 1½ cupfuls of crushed teaberry or wintergreen candy sticks. Continue to freeze the ice cream until it is set.

TOMATO ICE CREAM: In a saucepan, over gentle heat, simmer 6 large ripe tomatoes, chopped coarse, until they are of a pasty consistency; strain them. Make the custard with 1 cupful of light cream; to the hot custard, add the tomato purée and 1 six-ounce can of tomato paste. Into the chilled custard, before adding the heavy cream, stir 1 teaspoonful of vanilla extract. Complete the basic recipe as written.

# A Few Sauces and Salads

# A Few Sauces and Salads

## Basil Sauce*

*For main-dish soufflés and mousses*

YIELD: ABOUT 1½ CUPS (RECIPE MAY BE DOUBLED AND REFRIGERATED)
PREPARATION: 10 MINUTES

    1 cup Mayonnaise, page 189
    ⅓ cup light cream
    ⅓ cup fresh basil leaves, tightly packed, the stems removed,
        rinsed, and dried on absorbent paper
    Salt

In the container of a food processor or blender, combine the mayonnaise, cream, and basil leaves. Whirl them until the mixture is smooth. Adjust the seasoning with salt to taste.

## Cucumber Sauce

*For main-dish soufflés and mousses*

YIELD: ABOUT 3 CUPS (RECIPE MAY BE DOUBLED AND REFRIGERATED)
PREPARATION: 25 MINUTES (DOES NOT INCLUDE "WORKING" TIME IN THE REFRIGERATOR)

    2 medium-size cucumbers, peeled, seeded, and grated
    1½ teaspoons salt

In a mixing bowl, blend the cucumber and salt. Transfer the mixture to a colander, cover it with a heavy plate, and allow it to drain for 30 minutes.

* Many of the recipes in this section originally appeared in A *Celebration of Vegetables* (Atheneum, 1977); they are repeated in this book because they are particularly complementary to soufflés, mousses, jellies, and creams.

1 medium-size onion, peeled and grated
2 cups sour cream
2 teaspoons dried dill weed
A few drops of Tabasco sauce

In a mixing bowl, combine the drained cucumber, onion, sour cream, and dill weed. Blend the mixture well and add a little Tabasco to taste. Place the sauce in the refrigerator and allow it to "work" for 3 hours before serving it.

*Variation:*

DILL SAUCE: Omit the first step, above; make a sauce from the ingredients and directions in the second step, seasoning it with a little salt to taste.

## Hollandaise Sauce

*For main-dish mousses*

YIELD: ABOUT 1 CUP (RECIPE MAY BE DOUBLED)
PREPARATION: 10 MINUTES

Have all the ingredients at room temperature.

3 egg yolks
2 tablespoons strained fresh lemon juice
2 tablespoons water
¼ teaspoon salt
A drop or two of Tabasco sauce

In the container of a food processor or blender, combine the egg yolks, lemon juice, water, salt, and Tabasco sauce. Whirl the ingredients briefly to blend them well.

¼ pound (1 stick) sweet butter, melted and brought just
    to the boil

With the motor running, add the bubbling butter in a slow steady stream. Turn off the motor when all the butter is poured.

If you are holding the sauce for serving later, transfer it to the top of a small double boiler and, just before serving, heat it over gently simmering water.

## Mayonnaise

*For composed salads and for use as a garnish*

YIELD: ABOUT 1¼ CUPS (RECIPE MAY BE DOUBLED AND REFRIGERATED)
PREPARATION: 10 MINUTES

Have all the ingredients at room temperature.

1 egg *or* 2 egg yolks
¼ cup fine olive oil *or* vegetable oil
2 teaspoons cider vinegar *or* 3 tablespoons strained fresh lemon juice

¾ teaspoon Dijon-style mustard
½ teaspoon salt

In the container of a food processor or blender, combine the egg, oil, vinegar, mustard, and salt. Whirl the ingredients briefly to blend them well.

¾ cup fine olive oil *or* vegetable oil

With the motor running, add the second quantity of oil in a thin steady stream. Turn off the motor when all the oil is poured.

Transfer the mayonnaise to a jar with a tight-fitting lid and refrigerate it.

*Variations:*

AIOLI SAUCE: Add 1 or 2 cloves garlic, peeled and coarsely chopped, to the ingredients in step one (above).

CURRY MAYONNAISE: Prepare the recipe above as written; add to the finished mayonnaise, curry powder to taste (½ to 1 teaspoonful, depending upon the strength of flavor you desire); using a fork, beat the sauce to blend it well.

GREEN MAYONNAISE: To the ingredients in step one, above, add ½ cupful of coarse-chopped parsley, 1 cupful of coarse-chopped raw spinach, 3 scallions, chopped, and ½ teaspoonful of sugar; blend the mixture well before proceeding with step two. If desired, watercress may be substituted for the spinach. Green mayonnaise is piquant and decorative and goes well with cold main-dish mousses.

## Mayonnaise-and-Lemon Sauce

*For hot main-dish mousses*

YIELD: ABOUT 1¼ CUPS (RECIPE MAY BE DOUBLED AND REFRIGERATED)
PREPARATION: 15 MINUTES

Have all the ingredients at room temperature.

    1 cup Mayonnaise, page 189
    2 eggs
    Strained juice of 1 medium-size lemon
    ½ teaspoon Dijon-style mustard
    ½ teaspoon salt

In a mixing bowl, beat together the mayonnaise, eggs, lemon juice, mustard, and salt. When they are well blended, transfer the mixture to a saucepan and, over gentle heat, cook it, stirring constantly, until it thickens; do not let it boil. Strain it into a serving dish or refrigerator container.

To reheat the sauce, transfer it to the top of a double boiler over simmering water.

## Vinaigrette Sauce

*For all green and vegetable salads*

YIELD: ABOUT 1 CUP
PREPARATION: 5 MINUTES

    1 teaspoon salt
    1 teaspoon sugar
    ½ teaspoon white pepper
    1 teaspoon Dijon-style
      mustard

    2 tablespoons water
    4 tablespoons vinegar
      of your choice

In a jar with a tight-fitting lid, combine and shake together the salt, sugar, pepper, mustard, water, and vinegar until the salt and sugar are dissolved.

    ¾ cup fine olive oil

To the contents of the jar, add the olive oil and shake the mixture until it is thoroughly blended.

## Berry Sauce

*For hot and cold fruit-based dessert soufflés*

YIELD: ABOUT 1¼ CUPS (RECIPE MAY BE DOUBLED AND REFRIGERATED)
PREPARATION: 10 MINUTES
CHILLING TIME: 3 HOURS

    1 pint raspberries or strawberries, rinsed
    Sugar
    Salt

Into a mixing bowl, sieve the berries. Season the purée to taste with sugar and a few grains of salt. Chill the sauce before serving it.

## Brandy-and-Lemon Sauce

*For desserts, hot and cold dessert soufflés, and dessert mousses*

YIELD: ABOUT 1½ CUPS (RECIPE MAY BE DOUBLED AND REFRIGERATED)
PREPARATION: 10 MINUTES

⅔ cup Cognac
¼ cup strained fresh lemon juice
¾ teaspoon ground ginger
⅔ cup honey

In a jar with a tight-fitting lid, combine the Cognac, lemon juice, ginger, and honey. Shake the ingredients vigorously to blend them well.

## Crème anglaise (Custard Sauce)

*For desserts*

YIELD: 2½ CUPS (RECIPE MAY BE DOUBLED AND REFRIGERATED, BUT FOR A FEW DAYS ONLY)
PREPARATION: 15 MINUTES

Have all the ingredients at room temperature

⅔ cup sugar
½ teaspoon cornstarch
4 egg yolks, lightly beaten
A pinch of salt

Mix the sugar with the cornstarch. In the top of a double boiler, combine the sugar-cornstarch mixture, egg yolks, and salt.

2 cups milk, scalded

Into the contents of the double boiler, stir the milk. Over simmering water, cook the custard, stirring, until it coats the metal spoon.

1 teaspoon vanilla extract *or* cream sherry

Allow the sauce to cool slightly before stirring in the seasoning of your choice.

To prevent the *crème anglaise* from "crusting," store it in the refrigerator with plastic wrap pressed onto the surface of the sauce.

*Variations:*

ORANGE CUSTARD SAUCE: Omit the vanilla or sherry and to the hot custard, add ¼ cupful of strained fresh orange juice, and 1 tablespoonful of orange-flavored liqueur. This sauce will be thinner than *crème anglaise*.

PORT WINE CUSTARD SAUCE: Reduce the milk to 1½ cupfuls and add ½ cupful of white port wine; omit the vanilla or sherry and season the sauce with the strained juice and grated rind of 1 small lemon.

If, while you are preparing them, any of these sauces curdle, transfer the mixture to the container of an electric blender and whirl it until it is smooth; the resultant sauce will be thinner than if it had not curdled, but the flavor will be the same.

## Apple, Celery, and Green Pea Salad

6 SERVINGS (RECIPE MAY BE DOUBLED AND REFRIGERATED)
PREPARATION: 30 MINUTES
CHILLING TIME: 3 HOURS

*A fresh-tasting complement to cold main-dish mousses and aspics.*

| | |
|---|---|
| 4 large tart apples, peeled, cored, diced fine, and tossed with the strained juice of 1 medium-size lemon | 2 cups celery, diced fine |
| | ½ small green pepper, seeded and chopped fine |
| 2 nine-ounce packages frozen *small* peas, fully thawed to room temperature | 1 small onion, peeled and grated |
| | Mayonnaise, page 189 |

Drain the juice from the apples and combine them in a mixing bowl, with the peas, celery, pepper, and onion. Fold the ingredients with sufficient mayonnaise to bind them.

Salt
White pepper

Adjust the seasoning to taste. Chill the salad for at least 3 hours before serving it.


## Bulgur Salad

A *piquant complement to cold main-dish mousses; serve also as a separate salad with aspics.*

6 SERVINGS (RECIPE MAY BE DOUBLED AND REFRIGERATED)
PREPARATION: 30 MINUTES (THE PREPARATION TIME DOES NOT INCLUDE
PREPARING THE BULGUR)
CHILLING TIME: 3 HOURS

Bulgur, bulghur, or cracked wheat, is available at specialty food shops and increasingly in supermarkets.

When fresh mint is unavailable, use 2 teaspoonfuls dried mint, ground to a powder in a mortar with pestle.

> 2 cups coarse bulgur
> 6 cups boiling salted water

In a mixing bowl, combine the bulgur and boiling water; allow the grain to stand, covered, until the water is cool. Drain it thoroughly and then press out any excess moisture.

> 12 scallions, trimmed and chopped, with as much green as is
>     crisp
> 1 cup fine-chopped parsley
> 3 medium-size ripe tomatoes, peeled, seeded, and chopped
> ⅓ cup fine olive oil
> Grated rind and strained juice of 1 medium-size lemon
> ½ cup fine-chopped fresh mint leaves

In a mixing bowl, combine the drained bulgur with the scallions, parsley, tomatoes, olive oil, lemon rind and juice, and mint leaves. Toss the mixture to blend it well. Additional olive oil and lemon juice may be used, if desired. Chill the salad for at least 3 hours before serving it.

## Chicken Salad

*To accompany main-dish mousses and aspics*

6 TO 8 SERVINGS
PREPARATION: 30 MINUTES
CHILLING TIME: 3 HOURS

This recipe may also be used to make Ham, Turkey, or Shrimp Salad; merely substitute for the chicken the same quantity of ham, turkey, or shrimp.

> **2 cups diced cooked chicken meat**
> **Strained juice of 1 medium lemon**

In a mixing bowl, toss the chicken with the lemon juice and allow it to stand, covered, for 1 hour.

> **¾ cup Mayonnaise, page 189**
> **3 ribs celery, diced, *or* 1 five-ounce can water chestnuts, drained and sliced thin**
> **¼ cup fine-chopped sweet pickle (optional)**
> **Salt**
> **White pepper**

To the chicken, add the mayonnaise, celery, and pickle; blend the mixture well. Season the salad with salt and pepper to taste.

*Variations:*

Chicken Salad can and should give room for culinary creativeness; therefore, try adding one or more for the following:

> **6 scallions, trimmed and sliced thin, with some of the crisp green**
> **1 five-ounce can bamboo shoots, drained and diced**
> **¼ cup green pepper, seeded and diced (*or* sweet red pepper)**
> **¼ cup pimiento, chopped**
> **2 or 3 tablespoons crystallized ginger, chopped fine**
> **1 teaspoon (or more, to taste) prepared horseradish**
> **½ cup heavy cream, whipped**
> **¾ cup sour cream, in place of the mayonnaise**

Fine-chopped parsley (as much as you like)
1 or 2 teaspoons any fresh herb of your choice, chopped fine
½ cup frozen tiny peas, fully thawed to room temperature

These are only a few ideas; enjoy yourself by trying some of your own.

## Egg Salad

*To accompany main-dish mousses and aspics*

6 SERVINGS

PREPARATION: 45 MINUTES (INCLUDES HARD-COOKING THE EGGS, 15 MINUTES)

CHILLING TIME: 3 HOURS

| | |
|---|---|
| 8 to 10 hard-cooked eggs, chilled and peeled | ½ cup Mayonnaise, page 189 |
| ¼ cup thin-sliced scallions | Salt |
| ¼ cup fine-chopped sweet gherkins | White pepper |

Cut the eggs into fairly large pieces. In a mixing bowl, combine and blend the scallions, sweet gherkins, and mayonnaise. Fold in the prepared eggs. Season the salad to taste.

*Variations:*

You may omit the scallions and/or sweet gherkins and use in their place one or more of the following:

1 medium red onion, peeled and chopped fine
½ cupful of diced celery
1 five-ounce can of water chestnuts, sliced
¼ to ½ cupful of fine-chopped parsley
¼ to ½ cupful of fine-chopped watercress leaves
¼ cupful of fine-chopped green or sweet red pepper
1 three-ounce jar pimientos, chopped fine
1 five-ounce can of bamboo shoots, chopped
1 ten-ounce package frozen tiny green peas, fully thawed to room temperature (especially helpful if you want to "stretch" the salad)

Most important: Use only sufficient mayonnaise to bind the mixture; egg salad made with excess mayonnaise does not do well as a filler for ring molds, nor does it contain itself attractively on the plate.

## Mixed Vegetable Salad

*To accompany main-dish mousses and aspics*

6 SERVINGS (MAY BE DOUBLED AND REFRIGERATED)
PREPARATION: 20 MINUTES

**2 or 3 ten-ounce packages frozen mixed vegetables**

Cook the vegetables according to the directions on the package; do not overcook them. Refresh them in cold water and drain them thoroughly.

**Mayonnaise, page 189**
**Salt**
**Fresh-ground pepper**

In a mixing bowl, combine the vegetables with sufficient mayonnaise to bind them. Season the salad to taste.

The salad may also be made with any of the mayonnaise-based sauces: alioli, curry mayonnaise, or green mayonnaise, page 190.

## Kumquats Prepared for Cooking

YIELD: ABOUT 3 CUPS (RECIPE MAY BE DOUBLED, REFRIGERATED, AND FROZEN)
PREPARATION: 45 MINUTES

**2 quarts ripe kumquats, stemmed and rinsed**

Cut the kumquats in half crosswise; into a saucepan, squeeze the pulp; in a second saucepan, collect the rinds.

**Water**

To the contents of each saucepan, add sufficient water just to start to the boil. Simmer the pulp and rinds, covered, for 30 minutes, or until they are very tender; stir them often.

Strain the pulp, discarding the seeds and residue. In the container of a food processor or blender, whirl the rinds with their liquid until they are reduced to a purée (it will not be entirely smooth).

**Salt**
**Sugar**

Measure the strained pulp and purée into a mixing bowl. For each 2 cups, add a pinch of salt and ⅓ cupful of sugar (or more, to taste). Stir the mixture to blend it well and to dissolve the sugar. Store the prepared kumquats in jars or plastic containers in the refrigerator or freezer.

# Index

Key: (c) = cold; (d) = dessert; (h) = hot; (m) = main-dish (the key is used when the name of a dish does not adequately identify it)

aioli sauce, 189
almonds(s)
  chicken mousse with (c), 53
  cream, 157
  ice cream, 178
  milk jelly, 149
  soufflé (hd), 69
anchovy soufflé, 16
apple(s)
  Bavarian cream, 161
  and blackberry mousse (cd), 96
  -butter soufflé (c), 87
  -butter soufflé (h), 76
  celery, and green pea salad, 193
  cream, 158
  and horseradish mousse (c), 61
  mousse (cd), 95
  and onion soufflé, 18
  -sauce mousse (cd), 107
  soufflé (cd), 84
  soufflé (hd), 74, 81
  and yogurt pudding, 146
apricot
  gelatin, 141
  ice cream, 178
  mousse (cd), 94, 96
  preserve soufflé (c), 87
  preserve soufflé (h), 76
  soufflé (h), 69, 81
artichoke
  mousse (c), 50

mousse (h), 37
soufflé, 8
artichoke, Jerusalem
  mousse, 37
  soufflé, 29
asparagus
  mousse (c), 57
  soufflé, 8
  tips in aspic, 122
aspic(s) (main-dish jellies)
  basic recipe, 114
  defined, 111
  molds for, 113
    to line, 113
    to unmold, 112
  solid ingredients in, 113
    asparagus tips, 122
    avocado, 122
      with carrot, 122
    baba ghanouge, jellied, 130
    beans, kidney, 125
    beef, 122
    beets, 122
    broccoli, 123
    Brussels sprouts, 123
    cabbage, 123
    carrot, with avocado, 122
      and raisins, 123
    caviar with cucumber, 132
    chicken, 123
      salad with fruit, 123

aspic(s) (continued)
  citrus-based, 118
  clams, 124
  cottage cheese, 124
  crabmeat, 124
  cranberries, 131
  cream cheese, 124
  cucumber, 131
    with caviar, 132
    with yogurt, 124
  dates, with onion, 124
  eggs
    deviled, 125
    hard-cooked, 125
    in tarragon aspic, 132
  fish, 125
  fruit with chicken salad, 123
    with tuna, 128
  garnishes for, 120–121
  grapefruit and ham, 125
  grapes with sauerkraut, 127
  guacamole, 133
  ham, 125
    and grapefruit, 125
  hard-cooked eggs, 125
  herring, 125
  kidney beans, 125
  lamb, 126
  leeks, 125
  lemon, 118
  lentils, 126
  lettuce, 126
  lime, 118
  liver pâté, 126
  mint with split peas, 136
  orange, 119
  oysters, 134
  pâté, liver, 126
  pea, split, with mint, 136
  peppers, sweet, 129
  radishes, with sour cream, 127
  raisins, with carrot, 123
  salad
    chicken with fruit, 123
    shrimp, 127
    turkey, 129
  sauerkraut with grapes, 127
  scallops, 127
  seviche, 135
  shrimp, 127
    salad, 127
  sour cream with radishes, 127
  split peas with mint, 136
  sweetbreads, 128
  sweet peppers, 127
  tarragon aspic, eggs in, 132
  tomato, 119
  tripe, 137
  tuna, 128
    with fruit, 128
  turkey, 129
    salad, 129
  veal, 129
  vegetables
    mixed cooked, 129
    mixed raw, 129
    water chestnuts and watercress, 129
    yogurt with cucumber, 124
avocado
  in aspic, 122
  and carrot in aspic, 122
  cream (d), 159
  ice cream, 178
  mousse (cm), 49
    with shrimp (c), 48
  ring (cd), 145
  soufflé (cd), 84
  soufflé (hd), 81
  and watercress mousse (c), 49

baba ghanouge, jellied, 130
baked custard, 159
banana(s)
  Bavarian cream, 161
  ice cream, 178
  mousse (c), 97
  in orange gelatin, 143
  soufflé (c), 84
  soufflé (h), 70
  and yogurt pudding, 146
basil sauce, 187
Bavarian cream. See cream
bean, green
  mousse (h), 37
  soufflé, 12
bean, lima, mousse (c), 59
beans, kidney, in aspic, 125
béchamel
  defined, 4–5
  -based hot dessert soufflés, basic
      recipe, 68
beef
  in aspic, 122
  chipped, soufflé, 11
  liver mousse (h), 42
  stock, 115
beer, onion and cheese soufflé, 26
beet(s)
  in aspic, 122
  mousse (h), 37
  mousse (c), 50
  greens soufflé, 8
berry(ies)
  Bavarian cream, 162
  sauce, 191
  soufflé (h), black-, blue, rasp-,
      strawberry, 81
blackberry
  and apple mousse (cd), 96
  ice cream, 178
  mousse (c), 94
  preserve soufflé (c), 87
  preserve soufflé (h), 76
blancmange. See cream
blueberry
  ice cream, 178
  preserve soufflé (c), 87
  preserve soufflé (h), 76
  soufflé (c), 84

blue cheese
    mousse (c), 50
    and pear mousse (cd), 98
brandy
    Alexander soufflé (c), 85
    -and-lemon sauce, 192
Brie soufflé, 10
broccoli
    in aspic, 123
    mousse (h), 37, 46
    and salmon soufflé, 32
    soufflé, 8
brown stock, 115
Brussels sprout(s)
    in aspic, 123
    mousse (h), 37
    soufflé, 9
bulgur salad, 194
burnt cream, 167
    pumpkin, 168
burnt-sugar soufflé (c), 85
buttermilk cream, 166

cabbage in aspic, 123
calf's brains soufflé, 9
calf's liver mousse (h), 42
Camembert soufflé, 10
carrot(s)
    avocado with, in aspic, 122
    and raisins in aspic, 123
    mousse (h), 37
    soufflé (h), 9
    soufflé (cd), 85
cauliflower
    mousse (h), 38
    soufflé, 9
caviar, cucumber aspic with, 132
celeriac
    mousse (c), 51
    mousse (h), 37
    soufflé, 9
celery
    green pea, apple salad, 193
    soufflé, 10
celery root
    mousse (c), 51
    mousse (h), 37
    soufflé, 9
Charlotte russe, 164
Cheddar cheese
    mousse (c), 62
    soufflé (ed), 85
    soufflé (hm), 10
        with beer and onion, 26
cherry(ies)
    Bavarian cream, 161
    gelatin, 141
    mousse (c), 94
    preserve soufflé (c), 87
    preserve soufflé (h), 76
    soufflé (c), 85
    soufflé (h), 70
chestnuts
    ice cream, 179
    mousse (c), 99

soufflé (c), 92
soufflé (hm), 10
chicken
    in aspic, 123
    and clam soufflé, 10
    cornmeal soufflé with, 20
    liver mousse (h), 42
    liver mousse (c), 55
    liver soufflé, 10
    mousse (c), 52, 54, 59
        with almonds (c), 53
    mousse (h), 39
    salad, 195
        with fruit in aspic, 123
    soufflé, 10
    stock, 116
clarifying stock, 117
chipped beef soufflé, 11
chocolate
    Bavarian cream, 161
    blancmange, 168
    mousse (c), 100
    -orange mousse (c), 101
    soufflé (c), 85
    soufflé (h), 70, 75
chutney mousse (c), 102
citrus-based aspics, 118
clam(s)
    in aspic, 124
    chicken and, soufflé, 10
    and corn soufflé, 11
    mousse (c), 55
    soufflé, 11
coconut
    Bavarian cream, 161
    blancmange, 165
    milk jelly, 149
    mousse (c), 102
    soufflé (c), 85
coeur à la crème, 166
coffee
    Bavarian cream, 162
    pots de crème, 172
    soufflé (c), 86
    soufflé (h), 70
collard greens soufflé, 11
Concord grape soufflé (c), 86
corn
    clam and, soufflé, 11
    creamed, soufflé, 11
    fresh soufflé, 12
    mousse, 37
cornmeal soufflé, 19
    with chicken, 20
cottage cheese in aspic, 124
crab soufflé, 33
crabmeat in aspic, 124
cranberry(ies)
    in aspic, 131
    Bavarian cream, 162
    ice cream, 179
    mousse (c), 103, 106
cream-based hot dessert soufflés
    basic recipe, 68
cream cheese in aspic, 124

creamed corn soufflé, 11
creams
  and custards, defined, 155
    gelling time for, 156
    instructions for making, 155–156
    storing, 156
  almond, 157
  apple, 158
  avocado, 159
  baked custard, 159
  Bavarian cream(s)
    basic recipe, 160
    apple, 161
    banana, 161
    berry, 162
    cherry, 161
    chocolate, 161
    coconut, 161
    coffee, 162
    cranberry, 162
    fruit-based, 162
    ginger, 163
    hazelnut, 163
    guava, 162
    kumquat, 162
    lemon, 163
    lime, 163
    mango, 162
    mint, 163
    orange, 163
    papaya, 162
    peach, 162
    peanut brittle, 163
    pear, 162
    peppermint stick, 163
    persimmon, 162
    pineapple, 162
    pistachio, 163
    pomegranate-flavored, 164
    prune, 162
    quince, 162
    rose-flavored, 164
    rum, 164
  blancmange
    basic recipe, 164
    chocolate, 165
    coconut, 165
    fruit, 165
    lemon, 165
    orange, 165
  "boiled" custard, 156
  burnt pumpkin cream, 168
  buttermilk cream, 166
  Charlotte russe, 164
  coeur à la crème, 166
  coffee pots de crème, 172
crème anglaise, 156
  crème brûlée, 167
  custard
    baked, 159
    pumpkin, 172
  floating island, 168
  honey, 169
  lime, 169
  orange, 170

  port wine, 171
  pots de crème, 171
    blender-made, 172
    coffee, 172
  pumpkin
    burnt, 168
    custard, 172
    rose-water, 173
    Spanish, 164
    zabaglione, 174
    zuppa inglese, 175
crème anglaise (custard sauce), 192
  crème brûlée, 167
cucumber
  aspic, 131
    with caviar, 132
    with yogurt, 124
  mousse (c), 56
  sauce, 187
curry(ied)
  eggplant soufflé, 21
  mayonnaise, 189
custards. See cream
custard sauce (crème anglaise), 192
  orange, 193
  port wine, 193

Damson plum ice cream, 179
date(s)
  in aspic with onion, 124
  ice cream, 179
  soufflé (h), 70
deviled eggs in aspic, 125
dill sauce, 188
dried fruit mousse (c), 95

egg(s)
  deviled in aspic, 125
  hard-cooked in aspic, 125
  importance in soufflé, 3
  nutritive value, 3
  salad, 196
  in tarragon aspic, 132
  utensils for cooking, 4
  whites, beating of, 4
    storage, 4
eggnog soufflé (c), 86
eggplant
  curried, soufflé, 21
  mousse (h), 37

fennel soufflé, 12
fig(s)
  ice cream, 179
  Kadota, gelatin, 141
  soufflé (c), 86
fish
  in aspic, 125
  mousse (h), 41, 45
  soufflé, 12
  -roe soufflé, 14
floating island, 168
frozen strawberry mousse, 108
fruit
  in aspic, chicken salad with, 123
  -based Bavarian cream, 162

fruit (continued)
  *blancmange*, 165
  fresh, in gelatin, 141
  with tuna in aspic, 128

garlic mayonnaise, 189
garnishes for aspics, 120–121
gelatin
  to chill, 112
  to dissolve, 112
  history of, 111
  types of, 111
gelatin desserts
  basic recipe, 140
  general instructions, 139
  almond milk jelly, 149
  apple and yogurt pudding, 146
  apricot, 141
  avocado ring, 145
  banana and orange, 143
    and yogurt pudding, 146
  cherry, 141
  coconut milk jelly, 149
  fig, Kadota, 141
  fruit, fresh, 141
  ginger, 141
  grapes in white wine, 147
  guava, 141
  Kadota fig, 141
  kumquat, 142
  lemon, 142
  lime, 142
    and mint ring, 148
  litchis and loquats, 142
  mango, 142
  melon, 142
  milk jelly
    almond, 149
    coconut, 149
    orange-water, 150
    pistachio, 150
    rose-water, 149
  mincemeat, 143
  mint, fresh, 143
    and lime ring, 148
  orange, 143
    and banana, 143
    -water milk jelly, 150
  papaya, 143
  peach, 143
  pear, 144
  persimmon, 144
  pistachio milk jelly, 150
  plums, 144
    in red wine gelatin, 147
  port wine, 144
  prune, 144
    and yogurt pudding, 146
  quince, 144
  red wine, plums in, 147
  rhubarb, 144
  rose-water milk jelly, 149
  saffron pudding, 150
  sherry, 151
  strawberry, 145

tangerine, 145
white wine, grapes in, 147
wine
  red, plums in, 147
  white, grapes in, 147
yogurt
  and apple pudding, 146
  and banana pudding, 146
  and prune pudding, 146
ginger
  Bavarian cream, 163
  gelatin, 141
  ice cream, 129
  soufflé (*c*), 86
  soufflé (*h*), 70
Grand Marnier
  ice cream, 180
  soufflé (*c*), 87
  soufflé (*h*), 71
  with orange marmalade, 71
grape(s)
  preserve soufflé (*c*), 87
  preserve soufflé (*h*), 76
  with sauerkraut in aspic, 127
  in white wine gelatin, 147
grapefruit and ham in aspic, 125
green bean
  mousse (*h*), 37
  soufflé, 12
green mayonnaise, 190
green onion soufflé, 13
green pea
  apple, and celery salad, 193
  mousse (*h*), 37
  mousse (*c*), 57
  soufflé, 13
ground-meat soufflé, 23
*guacamole* in aspic, 133
guava
  Bavarian cream, 162
  gelatin, 141
  ice cream, 180
  soufflé (*c*), 87
  soufflé (*h*), 71

ham
  in aspic, 125
  and grapefruit in aspic, 125
  mousse (*c*), 59
  salad, 195
  and spinach soufflé, 15
hard-cooked eggs in aspic, 125
hazelnut
  Bavarian cream, 163
  soufflé (*h*), 71
herb, fresh, soufflé, 22
herring in aspic, 125
hollandaise sauce, 188
hominy soufflé, 24
honey
  cream, 169
  -flavored ice cream, 180
  mousse, 107
horseradish
  mousse (*c*), 60

horseradish (continued)
 and apple mousse, 61
 and spinach in aspic, 127

Ice cream(s)
 basic recipe, 176
 to freeze, 177–178
 almond, 178
 apricot, 178
 avocado, 178
 banana, 178
 blackberry, 178
 blueberry, 178
 chestnut, 179
 cranberry, 179
 Damson plum, 179
 date, 179
 fig, 179
 ginger, 179
 Grand Marnier, 180
 guava, 180
 honey-flavored, 180
 kumquat, 180
 lemon, 180
 mango, 180
 maple, 181
 mincemeat, 181
 mint, 181
 nesselrode, 181
 papaya, 181
 peach, 181
 peanut-brittle, 182
 pear, 182
 persimmon, 182
 pineapple, 182
 plum, Damson, 179
 prune, 182
 pumpkin, 183
 raisin, 183
 raspberry, 183
 rhubarb, 183
 strawberry, 183
 teaberry-stick, 183
 tomato, 184
 wintergreen-stick, 183

jam
 soufflé (c), 87
 soufflé (h), 76
jelly, main-dish. See aspics
Jerusalem artichoke
 mousse (h), 37
 soufflé, 29

Kadota fig gelatin, 141
kale soufflé, 13
kidney, lambs', mousse (h), 43
kidney beans in aspic, 125
kohlrabi mousse (h), 37
kumquat (s)
 Bavarian cream, 162
 gelatin, 142
 ice cream, 180
 mousse (c), 104
 preparation for cooking, 197

soufflé (c), 88
soufflé (h), 71

lamb
 in aspic, 126
 kidney mousse (h), 43
Laurette soufflé, 13
leeks in aspic, 125
lemon
 aspic, 118
 Bavarian cream, 163
 blancmange, 165
 brandy-and-, sauce, 192
 gelatin, 142
 ice cream, 180
 mayonnaise-and-, sauce, 190
 soufflé (c), 88
 soufflé (h), 71, 77
lentils in aspic, 126
lettuce
 in aspic, 126
 soufflé, 13
lima bean
 mousse (h), 37
 mousse (c), 59
lime
 aspic, 118
 Bavarian cream, 163
 cream, 169
 gelatin, 142
 marmalade soufflé (c), 87
 marmalade soufflé (h), 76
 and mint gelatin ring, 148
 soufflé (c), 88
 soufflé (h), 72
litchis and loquats in gelatin, 142
liver
 chicken
  mousse (c), 55
  soufflé, 10
 mousse (h), 42
 pâté
  in aspic, 126
  mousse (c), 63
  soufflé, 13
lobster soufflé, 33
loquats and litchis in gelatin, 142

macadamia nut soufflé (c), 88
macaroon
 soufflé (c), 88
 soufflé (h), 73
main-dish jellies. See aspics
mango
 Bavarian cream, 162
 gelatin, 142
 ice cream, 180
 mousse (c), 105
 soufflé (c), 88
maple ice cream, 181
 mousse (c), 106
 soufflé (c), 89
marmalade
 soufflé (c), 89
 soufflé (h), 76

mayonnaise, 189
  curry, 189
  garlic (aoli), 189
  green, 190
  and lemon sauce, 190
meat, ground
  soufflé, 23
  mousse (leftover meats), 43
melon
  gelatin, 142
  mousse (c), 94
  soufflé (c), 89
milk jelly
  almond, 149
  coconut, 149
  orange-water, 150
  pistachio, 150
  rose-water, 149
mincemeat
  gelatin, 143
  ice cream, 181
  mousse (c), 107
  soufflé (h), 72
mint
  Bavarian cream, 163
  -flavored soufflé (c), 89
  fresh, gelatin, 143
  ice cream, 181
  and lime gelatin ring, 148
  split pea aspic with, 136
mixed vegetable
  mousse (c), 65
  salad, 197
mocha soufflé (c), 89
molasses soufflé (c), 89
mousse(s), cold dessert
  basic recipe, fruit mousse, 93
  apple, 95
    and blackberry, 96
    -sauce, 107
  apricot, 94, 96
  banana, 97
  blackberry, 94
    and apple, 96
  blueberry, 94
  blue cheese and pear, 98
  cherry, 94
  chestnut, 99
  chocolate, 100
    and orange, 101
  chutney, 102
  coconut, 102
  cranberry, 103, 106
  dried fruit, 95
  frozen strawberry, 108
  honey, 107
  kumquat, 104
  mango, 105
  maple, 106
  melon, 94
  mincemeat, 107
  orange, 94
    and chocolate, 101
  peach, 95

pear, 95
  and blue cheese, 98
pineapple, 95
plum, 95
prune, 95
pumpkin, 95
raspberry, 95
strawberry, 95
  frozen, 108
mousse(s), cold main-dish
  gelling time, 47
  unmolding, 47
  almonds, chicken with, 53
  apple and horseradish, 61
  artichoke, 50
  asparagus, 57
  avocado, 49
    with shrimp, 48
    with watercress, 49
  bean, lima, 59
  beet, 50
  blue cheese, 50
  celeriac (celery root), 51
  cheese, Cheddar, 62
  chicken, 52, 54, 59
    with almonds, 53
    liver, 55
  clam, 55
  cucumber, 56
  green pea, 57
  ham, 59
  horseradish, 60
    and apple, 61
  lima bean, 59
  liver, chicken, 55
  mixed vegetables, 65
  pâté, liver, 63
  pea, green, 57
  roe, salmon, 63
  saffron rice, 61
  salad, Waldorf, 67
  salmon, 62
    roe, 63
  shrimp, 63
    with avocado, 48
  spinach, 64
  sweetbread, 66
  tongue, 60
  tuna, 63
  vegetable, mixed, 65
  Waldorf salad, 67
  watercress, avocado with, 49
mousse(s), hot main-dish
  general instructions, 5–6
  artichoke
    heart, 37
    Jerusalem, 37
  bean, green, 37
  beef liver, 42
  beet, 37
  broccoli, 37, 46
  Brussels sprouts, 37
  carrot, 37
  cauliflower, 38

mousse(s), hot main-dish (continued)
  celeriac (celery root), 37
  chicken, 39
    liver, 42
  corn, 37
  eggplant, 37
  fish, 41, 45
  green bean, 37
  green pea, 37
  Jerusalem artichoke, 37
  kidney, lamb's, 43
  kohlrabi, 37
  lamb's kidney, 43
  leftover meat, 43
  lima bean, 37
  liver
    beef, 42
    calf's, 42
  meat (leftover), 43
  mushroom, 36
    with spinach, 46
  parsnip, 37
  pea, green, 37
  pumpkin, 37
  salmon, 44
  spinach, 37, 45
    with mushrooms, 46
  squash
    summer, 37
    winter, 37
  tuna, 45
  turkey, 39
  turnip, 37
mushroom
  mousse (h), 36
  soufflé, 25
  and spinach mousse (h), 46
mustard green soufflé, 14

nutmeg soufflé (c), 89
nesselrode ice cream, 181

onion
  and apple soufflé, 18
  and cheese soufflé with beer, 26
  and dates in aspic, 124
  green, soufflé, 13
  soufflé, 14
orange
  aspic, 119
  Bavarian cream, 163
  blancmange, 165
  cream, 170
  custard sauce, 193
  gelatin, 143
    with bananas, 143
  marmalade
    soufflé (c), 87
      Grand Marnier with, 71
    soufflé (h), 76
  mousse (c), 94
    and chocolate, 101
  soufflé (c), 89
  soufflé (h), 72
  -water milk jelly, 150

oyster(s)
  in aspic, 134
  soufflé, 27

papaya
  Bavarian cream, 112
  gelatin, 143
  ice cream, 181
  soufflé (c), 89
parsnip
  mousse (h), 37
  soufflé, 35
pâté, liver
  in aspic, 126
  mousse (c), 63
  soufflé, 13
pea, green
  mousse (c), 57
  mousse (h), 37
  soufflé, 13
pea, split, aspic with mint, 136
peach
  Bavarian cream, 162
  gelatin, 143
  ice cream, 181
  mousse (c), 95
  preserve soufflé (c), 87
  preserve soufflé (h), 76
  soufflé (c), 90
  soufflé (h), 81
peanut brittle
  Bavarian cream, 163
  ice cream, 182
  soufflé (c), 90
pear
  Bavarian cream, 162
  and blue cheese mousse (cd), 98
  gelatin, 144
  ice cream, 182
  mousse (c), 98
  soufflé (c), 90
  soufflé (h), 81
peppers, sweet
  in aspic, 127
  soufflé, 15
peppermint-stick
  Bavarian cream, 163
  soufflé, 90
persimmon
  Bavarian cream, 162
  gelatin, 144
  ice cream, 182
  soufflé (c), 90
pineapple
  Bavarian cream, 162
  ice cream, 182
  mousse (c), 95
  preserve soufflé (c), 87
  preserve soufflé (h), 76
  soufflé (c), 90
pistachio
  Bavarian cream, 163
  milk jelly, 150
plum(s), Damson
  ice cream, 179

plum(s), Damson (continued)
  in gelatin, 144
  mousse (c), 95
  preserve soufflé (c), 87
  preserve soufflé (h), 76
  in red wine gelatin, 147
  soufflé (h), 81
pomegranate-flavored Bavarian cream,
    164
port wine
  cream, 171
  custard sauce, 193
  gelatin, 144
potato
  soufflé, 28
  sweet, soufflé, 29
  sweet, soufflé (hd), 79
pots de crème, 171
  blender-made, 172
  coffee, 172
provençale, soufflé, 30
prune
  Bavarian cream, 162
  -butter soufflé (c), 87
  -butter soufflé (h), 76
  gelatin, 144
  ice cream, 182
  mousse (c), 95
  soufflé (c), 90
  soufflé (h), 72
  and yogurt pudding, 146
pudding
  prune and yogurt, 146
  saffron, 150
pumpkin
  cream, burnt, 168
  custard, 172
  ice cream, 183
  mousse (cd), 95
  mousse (hm), 37
  soufflé (c), 91
  soufflé (h), 72
  spoon bread, 29

quince
  Bavarian cream, 162
  gelatin, 144
  soufflé (c), 91

radishes in aspic with sour cream, 127
raisin(s)
  in aspic with carrots, 123
  ice cream, 183
  soufflé (h), 72
raspberry
  ice cream, 183
  mousse (c), 95
  preserve soufflé (c), 87
  preserve soufflé (h), 76
red wine gelatin, plums in, 147
rhubarb
  gelatin, 144
  ice cream, 183
  soufflé (c), 91
rice, saffron, mousse (c), 61

ricotta soufflé (h), 78
ring, avocado (cd), 145
roe
  fish, soufflé, 14
  salmon mousse (c), 63
  shad, soufflé, 14
Roquefort soufflé, 14
rose-flavored Bavarian cream, 164
rosemary-flavored soufflé (c), 91
rose-water
  cream, 173
  milk jelly, 149
Rothschild soufflé (hd), 72
roux, defined, 4–5
rum
  Bavarian cream, 164
  soufflé (c), 91

saffron
  pudding, 150
  rice mousse (cm), 61
salad(s)
  apple, celery, and green pea, 193
  bulgur, 194
  chicken, 195
  egg, 196
  ham, 195
  shrimp, 195
  shrimp, in aspic, 127
  turkey, 195
  turkey in aspic, 129
  vegetable, mixed, 197
  Waldorf, mousse (m), 66
salmon
  and broccoli soufflé, 32
  mousse (c), 62
  mousse (h), 44
  soufflé, 31
  roe mousse (c), 63
Salzburger nockërln, 79
Sarah Bernhardt soufflé, 73
sardine soufflé, 17
sauces
  aioli, 189
  basil, 187
  berry, 191
  brandy-and-lemon, 192
  crème anglaise (custard), 192
  cucumber, 187
  curry mayonnaise, 189
  custard (crème anglaise), 192
    orange, 193
    port wine, 193
  dill, 188
  garlic mayonnaise, 189
  green mayonnaise, 190
  hollandaise, 188
  lemon
    brandy-and, 192
  mayonnaise-and, 190
  mayonnaise, 189
    aioli, 189
    curry, 189
    garlic, 189

sauces (continued)
    green, 190
    and lemon, 190
    orange custard, 193
    port wine custard, 193
    vinaigrette, 191
sauerkraut in aspic with grapes, 127
scallion (green onion) soufflé, 13
scallops
    in aspic, 127
    soufflé, 32
*seviche* in aspic, 135
shad roe soufflé, 14
sherry gelatin, 151
shrimp
    in aspic, 127
    and avocado mousse, 48
    salad, 195
        in aspic, 127
    mousse (*c*), 63
    soufflé, 33
soufflé(s), cold dessert
    basic recipe, 83
    dish for, 82
    apple, 84
        butter, 87
    apricot preserve, 87
    avocado, 84
    banana, 84
    blackberry preserve, 87
    blueberry, 84
        preserve, 87
    brandy Alexander, 85
    burnt sugar, 85
    carrot, 85
    cheese, 85
    cherry, 85
        preserve, 87
    chestnut, 92
    chocolate, 85
    coconut, 85
    coffee, 86
    Concord grape, 86
    eggnog, 86
    fig, 86
    ginger, 86
    Grand Marnier, 87
    grape preserve, 87
    guava, 87
    jam, 87
    kumquat, 88
    lemon, 88
    lime, 88
        marmalade, 87
    macadamia nut, 88
    macaroon, 88
    mango, 88
    maple, 89
    marmalade, 87
    melon, 89
    mint-flavored, 89
    mocha, 89
    molasses, 89
    nutmeg, 89

    orange, 89
        marmalade, 87
    papaya, 89
    peach, 90
        preserve, 87
    peanut brittle, 90
    pear, 90
    peppermint-stick, 90
    persimmon, 90
    pineapple, 90
        preserve, 87
    plum preserve, 87
    prune, 90
        butter, 87
    pumpkin, 91
    quince, 91
    raspberry preserve, 87
    rhubarb, 91
    rosemary-flavored, 91
    rum, 91
    spice, 91
    strawberry, 92
        preserve, 87
    tarragon-flavored, 92
    tutti-frutti, 92
    vanilla, 92
soufflé(s), hot dessert
    basic recipe for (*béchamel* or cream
        base), 68
    basic recipe for (fruit base), 80
    almond, 69
    apple, 74, 81
        butter, 76
    apricot, 69, 81
        preserve, 76
    avocado, 81
    banana, 70
    berry (black-, blue, rasp-,
        strawberry), 81
    blackberry preserve, 76
    cherry, 70
        preserve, 76
    chocolate, 70, 75
    coffee, 70
    date, 70
    ginger, 70
    Grand Marnier, 71
        with orange marmalade, 71
    grape preserve, 76
    guava, 71
    hazelnut, 71
    jam, 76
    kumquat, 71
    lemon, 71, 77
    lime, 72
        marmalade, 76
    macaroon, 73
    marmalade, 76
    mincemeat, 72
    orange, 72
        marmalade, 76
            Grand Marnier with, 71
    peach preserve, 76
    pear, 81
    pineapple preserve, 76

soufflé(s), hot dessert (continued)
  plum, 81
    preserve, 76
  potato, sweet, 79
  prune, 72
    butter, 76
  pumpkin, 72
  raisin, 72
  raspberry preserve, 76
  ricotta, 78
  Rothschild, 72
  Salzburger nockërln, 79
  Sarah Bernhardt, 73
  spice, 73
  strawberry, 73
    preserve, 76
  sweet potato, 79
  tutti frutti, 72
  vanilla, 73
soufflé(s), main-dish
  baking times, 6
  basic recipe for, 7
  making of, 5–6
  anchovy, 16
  apple and onion, 8
  artichoke, 8
    Jerusalem, 29
  asparagus, 8
  bean, green, 12
  beef, chipped, 11
  beer, onion and cheese with, 26
  beet greens, 8
  Brie, 10
  broccoli, 8
    salmon and, 32
  Brussels sprouts, 9
  calf's brain, 9
  Camembert, 10
  carrot, 9
  cauliflower, 9
  celeriac (celery root), 9
  celery, 10
  cheese, 10
    onion and, with beer, 26
  chestnut, 10
  chicken, 10
    and clam, 10
    cornmeal with, 20
    liver, 10
  chipped beef, 11
  clam, 11
    chicken and, 10
    corn and, 11
  collard greens, 11
  corn, clam and, 11
    creamed, 11
    fresh, 12
  cornmeal, 19
    with chicken, 20
  crab, 33
  creamed corn, 11
  curried eggplant, 21
  eggplant, curried, 21
  fennel, 12

  fish, 12
    roe, 14
  fresh corn, 12
  fresh herb, 22
  green bean, 12
  green onion, 13
  green pea, 13
  ground meat, 23
  ham, spinach and, 15
  herb, fresh, 22
  hominy, 24
  Jerusalem artichoke, 29
  kale, 13
  Laurette, 13
  lettuce, 13
  liver, chicken, 10
    pâté, 13
  lobster, 33
  meat, ground, 23
  mushroom, 25
  mustard greens, 14
  onion, 14
    apple and, 18
    cheese and, with beer, 26
    green, 13
  oyster, 27
  parsnip, 35
  pâté, liver, 13
  pea, green, 13
  pepper, sweet, 15
  potato, 28
    sweet, 29
  *provençale*, 30
  pumpkin spoon bread, 29
  roe
    fish, 14
    shad, 14
  Roquefort, 14
  salmon, 31
    with broccoli, 32
  sardine, 17
  scallion (green onion), 13
  scallop, 32
  shad roe, 14
  shrimp, 33
  spinach, 14
    and ham, 15
  spoon bread, 19
    pumpkin, 29
  squash
    summer, 15
    winter, 16
  sweetbread, 15
  sweet pepper, 15
  sweet potato, 29
  tomato, 34
  tuna, 32
  turkey, 15
  turnip, 35
  watercress, 16
  winter squash, 16
  zucchini, 16
*soufflé aux marrons* (cd), 92
  *provençale*, 30

*soufflé aux marrons* (*cd*) (continued)
   Rothschild, 72
   Sarah Bernhardt, 73
sour cream with radishes in aspic, 127
Spanish cream, 164
spice soufflé (*c*), 91
spice soufflé (*h*), 73
spinach
   in aspic with horseradish, 127
   mousse (*c*), 64
   mousse (*h*), 37, 45
      with mushrooms, 46
   soufflé, 14
      and ham, 15
split pea aspic with mint, 136
spoon bread, 19
   pumpkin, 29
squash
   summer, mousse, 37
   soufflé, 15
   winter
      mousse, 37
      soufflé, 16
stock
   beef, 115
   brown, 115
   chicken, 116
   to clarify, 117
   veal, 117
   vegetable, 117
   white, 117
strawberry
   gelatin, 145
   ice cream, 183
   mousse (*c*), 95
      frozen, 108
   preserve soufflé (*c*), 87
   preserve soufflé (*h*), 76
   soufflé (*c*), 92
   soufflé (*h*), 73
summer squash
   mousse, 37
   soufflé, 15
sweetbread(s)
   in aspic, 128
   mousse (*c*), 66
   soufflé, 15
sweet pepper(s)
   in aspic, 127
   soufflé, 15
sweet potato
   soufflé (*hd*), 79
   soufflé (*hm*), 29

tangerine gelatin, 145
tarragon
   aspic, eggs in, 132
   -flavored soufflé (*c*), 92
teaberry-stick ice cream, 183

tomato
   aspic, 119
   ice cream, 184
   soufflé, 34
tongue mousse (*c*), 60
tripe in aspic, 137
tuna
   in aspic, 128
   with fruit, 128
   mousse (*c*), 63
   mousse (*h*), 45
   soufflé, 32
turkey
   in aspic, 129
   mousse (*h*), 39
   salad, 195
      in aspic, 129
      soufflé, 15
turnip
   mousse (*h*), 37
   soufflé, 35
tutti frutti soufflé (*c*), 92
tutti frutti soufflé (*h*), 72

vanilla soufflé (*c*), 92
vanilla soufflé (*h*), 73
veal
   in aspic, 129
   stock, 117
vegetable(s), mixed
   cooked, in aspic, 129
   raw, in aspic, 129
   mousse (*c*), 65
   salad, 197
   stock, 117
vinaigrette sauce, 191

Waldorf salad mousse (*m*), 67
water chestnuts and watercress in aspic,
   129
watercress
   and avocado mousse (*cm*), 49
   and water chestnuts in aspic, 130
   soufflé, 16
white stock, 117
wine, white, gelatin, grapes in, 147
wintergreen-stick ice cream, 183
winter squash
   mousse, 37
   soufflé, 16

yogurt
   and apple pudding, 146
   and banana pudding, 146
   and cucumber in aspic, 124
   and prune pudding, 146

zabaglione, 174
zucchini soufflé, 16
*zuppa inglese*, 175